Anti-inflammatory Cookbook with Pictures

1000 Days Healthy and Delicious Anti-inflammatory Recipes for Busy People to Heal the Immune System and Reduce Inflammation

Fernando K. Rankin

Copyright© 2021 - Fernando K. Rankin All rights reserved.

The content contained within this book may not be reproduced, duplicated or transmitted without direct written permission from the author or the publisher.

Under no circumstances will any blame or legal responsibility be held against the publisher, or author, for any damages, reparation, or monetary loss due to the information contained within this book, either directly or indirectly.

Legal Notice:

This book is copyright protected. It is only for personal use. You cannot amend, distribute, sell, use, quote or paraphrase any part, or the content within this book, without the consent of the author or publisher.

Disclaimer Notice:

Please note the information contained within this document is for educational and entertainment purposes only. All effort has been executed to present accurate, up to date, reliable, complete information. No warranties of any kind are declared or implied. Readers acknowledge that the author is not engaged in the rendering of legal, financial, medical or professional advice. The content within this book has been derived from various sources. Please consult a licensed professional before attempting any techniques outlined in this book.

By reading this document, the reader agrees that under no circumstances is the author responsible for any losses, direct or indirect, that are incurred as a result of the use of the information contained within this document, including, but not limited to, errors, omissions, or inaccuracies.

CONTENT

Introduction   1

Chapter 1 Breakfasts   7

Chapter 2 Vegetarian Mains   16

Chapter 3 Vegetables and Sides   24

Chapter 4 Beef, Pork, and Lamb   33

Chapter 5 Poultry   42

Chapter 6 Fish and Seafood   51

Chapter 7 Salads   60

Chapter 8 Desserts   70

Chapter 9 Staples, Sauces, Dips, and Dressings   80

Chapter 10 Snacks and Appetizers   87

Conclusion   94

Appendix 1 Measurement Conversion Chart   95

Appendix 2 The Dirty Dozen and Clean Fifteen   96

Introduction

A great number of people around the world suffer from inflammation in their bodies on a daily basis. It often remains undiagnosed and yet, it is quite dangerous to health. I truly believe that this is something that we should talk about more. Chronic inflammatory diseases are one of the biggest causes of death in the world, with the World Health Organization ranking them as the biggest threat to human health (Pahwa et al., 2019).

I first started my journey of inflammation discovery to help my mother who suffers from an autoimmune disease called psoriasis.

Psoriasis is a hereditary autoimmune disease that causes the immune system to overproduce skin cells. For someone without this condition, the skin cells usually complete their cycle—grow and then fall off—in about a month. For someone with psoriasis, this cycle is sped up to around four days. The skin cells also don't always fall off and tend to build up and form what look like scales or dry flakes on the skin. This condition leads to high levels of inflammation, which negatively affects health, and can damage other tissues in the body as well as the organs.

I have seen how this disease has affected my mother's quality of life, and I am noticing symptoms in myself more and more. Sadly, we are not alone, as countless other people suffer from conditions associated with chronic inflammation, and they are tired of hearing *but you don't look sick*. So, I set out to learn everything there is to know about inflammation and how to manage it.

Once I started my research, I was shocked to learn about the wide range of issues that inflammation can cause. And not only to those suffering from an existing condition, but for most people living in the modern world. Chronic inflammation can be a silent killer when left untreated.

And that is why I am writing this book. I want to help anyone willing to make the necessary changes to reduce their risk of developing inflammatory disease. This book is also for anyone who would like to learn to eat mindfully to give their body the best chance of staying healthy.

Flummoxed by Inflammation

Inflammation is not all bad. It is actually a vital part of the body's defense mechanism and is very important to the healing process. However, sometimes things go haywire, and processes that are meant to help our bodies end up hurting them. This is the case with chronic inflammation.

What Is Inflammation?

Inflammation is the immune system's response to an irritation in the body. This irritation could be from an injury, illness, a foreign body such as a splinter, or a pathogen such as bacteria or a virus. The area becomes inflamed as the body tries to protect itself by bringing more blood, or removing the foreign body or pathogen, to start the healing process.

There are five indicators of inflammation. These are redness due to an increase in blood flow, swelling, pain, heat, and loss of function which refers to reduced mobility in the area. This is, however, not always the case as, sometimes inflammation does not present with any indicators.

There are two types of inflammation; namely, acute inflammation and chronic inflammation. Acute inflammation is a short-term event, for example, due to an injury. Chronic inflammation occurs long-term and can persist for months or, in extreme cases, for years. This prolonged inflammation can cause your immune system to attack your organs and healthy tissue, which is where the problem becomes more serious.

How Do I Know if I Have Inflammatory Issues?

There are a few factors that can increase the risk of inflammatory responses in your body. These factors include:

Diet: Saturated or trans fats—which are found in dairy, red meat, baked goods, and fried foods—are associated with higher levels of inflammation-causing molecules in the body. The same is true for refined sugar and highly processed foods.

Age: As we get older, we produce more inflammation-causing molecules in our bodies.

Stress and sleep disorders: This is an important one to consider because stress is a big problem for many people around the world. Modern life has become extremely fast paced and can be very demanding on our health. Emotional and physical stress can cause increased production of inflammation-causing molecules. Irregular sleeping patterns can have the same effect.

Obesity: Studies have shown a connection between high levels of fatty tissue and the production of inflammation-causing molecules (Pahwa et al., 2019). Some of these studies have found that fat levels and inflammation-causing molecules increase proportionally.

Low levels of sex hormones: Hormones such as estrogen and testosterone have been found to inhibit the production of inflammation-causing molecules in our bodies. When the levels of these hormones are low, the suppressing effect cannot occur.

Smoking: Smoking cigarettes has been found to decrease the levels of inflammatory-fighting molecules which are needed to keep inflammation levels within a healthy range.

Chronic inflammation can also develop from sensitivity or long-term exposure to an irritant; for example, a chemical in the air.

The common symptoms of chronic inflammation include:

- weight loss or weight gain
- pain in the body

- mood swings, depression, and anxiety
- acid reflux, diarrhea, or constipation
- insomnia and chronic fatigue
- recurrent infections

Diagnosing chronic inflammation can be done with the help of a blood test. Unfortunately, these levels are usually only checked when there is another medical condition present that is causing inflammation. For this reason, many people suffer from chronic inflammation without ever being diagnosed.

What Damage Does Chronic Inflammation Cause?

Chronic inflammation is the cause of most chronic diseases and poses a huge threat to health. Prolonged inflammation can cause the body to mistake its own healthy tissue and organs as harmful and start to attack them, which can lead to a range of autoimmune diseases. According to Pahwa et al. (2019), it is also thought to be linked to other diseases which include:

Cancer: Inflammation plays a role in various types of cancers including ovarian, prostate, pancreatic, kidney, lung, hepatocellular, mesothelioma, and colorectal.

Alzheimer's disease: This presents more in older people as chronic inflammation over time has been shown to decrease cognitive function and can lead to dementia.

Cardiovascular disease: Chronic inflammation can lead to atherosclerosis, which is present when a fatty plaque that is full of cholesterol builds up inside the arteries. Your body can then mistake this plaque for a foreign substance and may respond with inflammation to try to stop the damage. This inflammation can lead to other serious cardiovascular issues such as a stroke.

Diabetes: High levels of body fat can cause chronic inflammation and that changes the way that insulin acts in the body by disrupting insulin-signaling pathways. This can lead to insulin resistance. Chronic inflammation has been said to be at the root of many complications associated with diabetes.

Chronic obstructive pulmonary disease (COPD): This is a lung disease that presents as a chronic inflammatory response to irritations in the lungs and can lead to long-term issues with breathing.

Rheumatoid arthritis: Those who are genetically predisposed to this condition may develop rheumatoid arthritis due to an autoimmune response to external irritants like smoking. This autoimmune response causes inflammation in the joints which, over time, can cause further complications.

Chronic kidney disease: Inflammation is a common part of this disease. It can lead to inflammation-

causing molecules in the blood which further aggravate the disease and can lead to death.

Allergic asthma: This is a chronic inflammatory disorder that can develop if the immune system overresponds and triggers inflammation and tissue remodeling in the airways.

Inflammatory bowel disease: This is a group of diseases that is associated with chronic inflammation of the digestive tract. This can start as ulcerative colitis which causes long-term inflammation as well as ulcers in the rectum or large intestine. Crohn's disease is one type of inflammatory bowel disease.

The Anti-Inflammatory Diet

This diet is really quite simple. In order to manage inflammation, you need to eat more anti-inflammatory foods and fewer inflammatory foods. You should try to combine a wide variety of foods that give your body lots of nutrients, healthy fats, and antioxidants. This is the concept of the anti-inflammatory diet in a nutshell.

The Anti-Inflammatory Diet Explained

There are certain foods that trigger inflammation and certain foods that help fight it. The anti-inflammatory diet discourages or limits the consumption of processed foods, foods with added sugar, red meats, and alcohol. Instead, it favors fruits and vegetables, foods containing omega-3 fatty acids, whole grains, lean protein, healthful fats, and spices. These inflammation-fighting foods provide us with plenty of antioxidants which are important because they help the body to remove free radicals. Our bodies naturally produce antioxidants to help remove the free radicals; however, sometimes they need a bit of help from dietary antioxidants as well. Free radicals are a byproduct of certain processes such as metabolism; however, the level of these in the body can be increased by external irritants such as stress or poor diet.

Principles of the Anti-Inflammatory Diet

The principles of this diet are not very complicated:

1. Eat less sugar: This one is very important to watch out for. When I refer to sugar here, I do not only mean actual sugar. Refined carbohydrates turn to sugar once they are in the body. Examples of refined carbohydrates include white bread, white rice, and French fries. According to the American Heart Association (2018), the daily intake of sugar for men is around nine teaspoons, and for women around six teaspoons. I know that chocolates and cookies are yummy, but we have to be strong and reach for some fruit instead.

2. Eat less dairy: Fermented dairy such as yogurt is fine to eat, but fresh dairy products can sometimes trigger inflammation.

3. Eat lots of fresh fruits and vegetables: These are so important for getting antioxidants into your system and are a great source of vitamins and fiber.

4. Eat foods that are high in Omega-3: We often don't get enough of this fatty acid in our diet. We get a large amount of Omega-6, since it is found in vegetable oils and processed food, but this needs to be balanced proportionally with Omega-3.

5. Stay away from processed foods: The anti-inflammatory diet is all about fresh and wholesome foods. I think we all realize that processed foods don't do much good for our bodies. Meal prepping will help you a lot in avoiding these foods.

The Do's and Don'ts

Do:
- Fill up with fiber: Peas, lentils, and beans are great sources of fiber.
- Spice up your life: There are many spices that can help to fight inflammation such as paprika, garlic, turmeric, and ginger.
- Swap refined carbohydrates for whole grains: Refined carbohydrates like those found in white bread, don't offer our bodies much fiber. Whole grains are loaded with fiber and other nutrients too.
- Keep it lean: Too much fat on your meat can trigger inflammation.
- Favor marine: Fatty fish is a great source of Omega-3. Examples of fatty fish include salmon, anchovies, tuna, sardines, and mackerel.
- Go nuts: A handful of nuts is all you need per day. They are loaded with healthy fats, fiber, and protein.
- Have your glass of red: There is a substance found in red wine called resveratrol that is thought to fight inflammation. It is, however, important to stick to one glass per day. People suffering from any disease should consult their doctor before indulging.

Don't:
- Reuse cooking oil: Cooking repeatedly with the same oil can cause free radicals to form in the body.
- Use too much olive oil: Although this is a healthy oil, too much of anything can be harmful. It is advised to use two to three tablespoons per day.
- Miss out on cocoa: Now, this is not an excuse to eat chocolate. Cocoa contains something called flavonoids which have been said to reduce inflammation. Avoid sugary foods that contain cocoa and rather try to incorporate it in other ways; for example, you can add it to your smoothies.
- Overlook your sugar intake: I know I've said this before, but I can't stress how important it is.
- Be too hard on yourself: Perfection is not the goal. Changes to the way you think about food are the goal. Don't give up because you had a bad day—just try to make better choices tomorrow.

Foods to Eat and Foods to Avoid

Foods to Eat	Foods to Avoid
Fresh fruits, especially berries	Processed snack foods like chips, crackers, and pretzels
Fresh vegetables, especially leafy greens, such as spinach, kale, and collards	Processed meats like hot dogs and sausages
Foods filled with Omega-3 fatty acids, such as extra-virgin olive oil, avocado oil and flaxseed oil	Foods with added sugar such as candy, cake, and cookies
Fiber-rich foods like lentils, peas, and beans	French fries and other fried foods
Fatty fish like salmon, mackerel, tuna, and sardines	Refined carbohydrates like white rice, white bread, and white pasta
Lean meat	Unhealthy oils like soybean and corn oil
Nuts and seeds like almonds, walnuts, chia seeds, and flaxseeds	Foods containing trans fats like margarine
Some herbs and spices like turmeric, ginger, and cinnamon	Large amounts of alcohol
Green and black tea	

Health Benefits

The health benefits of the anti-inflammatory diet are numerous.

1. Besides lowering inflammation, eating a diet like this has been shown to reduce bloating and help with weight management.

2. According to Sinha Dutta (2020), it reduces the risk of heart disease and strokes by a whopping 25%.

3. It can cut the risk of developing Parkinson's disease in half.

4. This diet can even reduce the risk of developing some cancers.

5. The increased intake of fiber regulates blood sugar levels and cholesterol levels which, in turn, lowers your risk of Alzheimer's disease as well as type 2 diabetes.

6. It can help fight depression by improving mood and energy levels.

7. The high amount of antioxidants from fresh fruits and vegetables contribute to anti-aging.

8. Eating such nutrient-rich foods also protects the muscles from damage and promotes healthy brain function, improved memory, and better concentration.

The anti-inflammatory diet can help to keep you feeling young and agile, both physically and mentally. All of these factors contribute to increased longevity and quality of life for anyone who follows this way of eating. Don't wait until you're sick to make a change, as this diet is for everyone.

Chapter 1 Breakfasts

1 **Mushroom "Frittata"** 9
2 **Simple Steel-Cut Oats** 9
3 **Sweet Potato Frittata** 9
4 **Avocado Boat Breakfast** 10
5 **Blueberry-Millet Breakfast Bake** 10
6 **Maple-Cinnamon Granola** 10
7 **Coconut Rice with Berries** 12
8 **Gluten-Free Vanilla Crepes** 12
9 **Meditteranean Vegetable Frittata** 12
10 **Smoked Salmon Scrambled Eggs** 14
11 **Mini Broccoli Frittatas** 14
12 **Wake Me Up Fruit Cereal** 14
13 **Chia Breakfast Pudding** 15
14 **Fruit-and-Seed Breakfast Bars** 15
15 **Maple-Tahini Oatmeal** 15

8 | Chapter 1: Breakfasts

Mushroom "Frittata"

Prep time: 15 minutes | Cook time: 20 minutes | Serves 6

1½ cups chickpea flour
1½ cups water
1 teaspoon salt
2 tablespoons extra-virgin olive oil
1 small red onion, diced
2 pints sliced mushrooms

1 teaspoon ground turmeric
½ teaspoon ground cumin
1 teaspoon salt
½ teaspoon freshly ground black pepper
2 tablespoons chopped fresh parsley

1. Preheat the oven to 350°F (180°C). 2. In a small bowl, slowly whisk the water into the chickpea flour; add the salt and set aside. 3. In a large cast iron or oven-safe skillet over high heat, add the olive oil. When the oil is hot, add the onion. Sauté for 3 to 5 minutes, until onion is softened and slightly translucent. Add the mushrooms and sauté for 5 minutes more. Add the turmeric, cumin, salt, and pepper, and sauté for 1 minute. 4. Pour the batter over the vegetables and sprinkle with the parsley. Place the skillet in the preheated oven and bake for 20 to 25 minutes. 5. Serve warm or at room temperature.

Per Serving
Calories: 240 | fat: 8g | protein: 11g | carbs: 34g | fiber: 10g | sugar: 7g | sodium: 792mg

Simple Steel-Cut Oats

Prep time: 15 minutes | Cook time: 6 to 8 hours | Serves 4 to 6

1 tablespoon coconut oil
4 cups boiling water
½ teaspoon sea salt

1 cup steel-cut oats
2 tablespoons blueberries

1. Coat the slow cooker with the coconut oil. 2. In your slow cooker, combine the boiling water, salt, and oats. 3. Cover the cooker and set to warm (or low if there is no warm setting). Cook for 6 to 8 hours, blueberry decorations and serve.

Per Serving
Calories: 172 | fat: 6g | protein: 6g | carbs: 27g | fiber: 4g | sugar: 0g | sodium: 291mg

Sweet Potato Frittata

Prep time: 15 minutes | Cook time: 30 minutes | Serves 4

tablespoon extra-virgin olive oil, plus more for brushing
1 large sweet potato, peeled and cut into 1-inch pieces
1 small red onion, chopped
1 teaspoon salt

¼ teaspoon freshly ground black pepper
1 teaspoon chopped fresh thyme leaves
8 large eggs, well beaten

1. Preheat the oven to 375°F (190°C). Brush a cast-iron skillet with a little olive oil. 2. Toss together the sweet potato and onion in the skillet. Drizzle with 1 tablespoon olive oil and add the salt and pepper. Bake until the potato is tender, 10 to 15 minutes. 3. Remove the skillet from the oven and sprinkle the thyme over the vegetables. Carefully pour the eggs over the vegetables and return the skillet to the oven. Bake until the eggs are firm and jiggle only slightly if you shake the skillet, about 15 minutes. 4. Let cool for at least 5 minutes before cutting into wedges and serving.

Per Serving
Calories: 220 | fat: 14g | protein: 15g | carbs: 9g | fiber: 1g | sugar: 2g | sodium: 760mg

Avocado Boat Breakfast

Prep time: 2 minutes | Cook time: 5 minutes | Serves 2

1 ripe avocado

2 free range eggs

1 tablespoon white wine vinegar

1. Place a large pan of water on a high heat and boil. 2. Once boiling add white wine vinegar (don't worry if you don't have it, it just helps with the poaching). 3. Lower the heat to a simmer and crack the eggs in. 4. Stir the water ever now and then around the eggs to keep them moving and cook for 2 minutes for a very runny yolk; 2 to 4 minutes for a soft to firm yolk and 5 for a hard yolk. 5. Whilst cooking, prepare your avocado by cutting through to the stone lengthways around the whole of the fruit. 6. Use your palms on each side to twist the avocado and it should come away into 2 halves. Using your knife, carefully wedge it into the stone and pull to remove the stone. Alternatively, cut around the stone with the knife and use the sharp end to coax it out. 7. Use your avocado halves as a dish for the eggs and serve.

Per Serving

Calories: 292 | fat: 24g | protein: 11g | carbs: 10g | fiber: 7g | sugar: 1g | sodium: 110mg

Blueberry-Millet Breakfast Bake

Prep time: 10 minutes | Cook time: 55 minutes | Serves 8

2 cups millet, soaked in water overnight

2 cups fresh or frozen blueberries

1¾ cups unsweetened applesauce

⅓ cup melted coconut oil

2 teaspoons grated fresh ginger

1½ teaspoons ground cinnamon

1. Preheat the oven to 350ºF (180ºC). 2. In a fine-mesh sieve, drain and rinse the millet for 1 to 2 minutes. Transfer to a large bowl. 3. Gently fold in the blueberries, applesauce, coconut oil, ginger, and cinnamon. 4. Pour the mixture into a 9-by-9-inch casserole dish. Cover with aluminum foil. 5. Place the dish in the preheated oven and bake for 40 minutes. Remove the foil and bake for 10 to 15 minutes more, or until lightly crisp on top.

Per Serving

Calories: 323 | fat: 13g | protein: 6g | carbs: 48g | fiber: 6g | sugar: 9g | sodium: 4mg

Maple-Cinnamon Granola

Prep time: 15 minutes | Cook time: 40 minutes | Serves 8

4 cups gluten-free rolled oats

1½ cups sunflower seeds

½ cup maple syrup

½ cup coconut oil

1½ teaspoons ground cinnamon

1. Preheat the oven to 325ºF (165ºC). 2. Line two baking sheets with parchment paper. 3. In a large bowl, stir together the oats, sunflower seeds, maple syrup, coconut oil, and cinnamon. Stir well so the oats and seeds are evenly coated with the syrup, oil, and cinnamon. 4. Divide the granola mixture evenly between the two sheets. 5. Place the sheets in the preheated oven and bake for 35 to 40 minutes, stirring every 10 minutes so everything browns evenly. 6. Cool completely, then store in large glass jars with tight-fitting lids.

Per Serving

Calories: 400 | fat: 22g | protein: 9g | carbs: 47g | fiber: 6g | sugar: 12g | sodium: 3mg

Coconut Rice with Berries

Prep time: 10 minutes | Cook time: 30 minutes | Serves 4

1 cup brown basmati rice
1 cup water
1 cup coconut milk
1 teaspoon salt

2 dates, pitted and chopped
1 cup fresh blueberries, or raspberries, divided
¼ cup toasted slivered almonds, divided
½ cup shaved coconut, divided

1. In a medium saucepan over high heat, combine the basmati rice, water, coconut milk, salt, and date pieces. 2. Stir until the mixture comes to a boil. Reduce the heat to simmer and cook for 20 to 30 minutes, without stirring, or until the rice is tender. 3. Divide the rice among four bowls and top each serving with ¼ cup of blueberries, 1 tablespoon of almonds, and 2 tablespoons of coconut.

Per Serving
Calories: 281 | fat: 8g | protein: 6g | carbs: 49g | fiber: 5g | sugar: 7g | sodium: 623mg

Gluten-Free Vanilla Crepes

Prep time: 5 minutes | Cook time: 10 minutes | Serves 2

2 free range eggs
1 teaspoon vanilla
½ cup nut milk of your choice
½ cup water

1 teaspoon maple syrup
1 cup gluten-free all-purpose flour
3 tablespoons coconut oil

1. In a medium bowl add the eggs, vanilla, nut milk, water, and syrup together until combined. Add the flour to the mix and whisk to combine to a smooth paste. 2. Take 2 tablespoons of the coconut oil and melt in a pan over a medium heat. 3. Add ½ crepe mixture and tilt and swirl the pan to form a round crepe shape. 4. Cook for about 2 minutes until the bottom is light brown and comes away from the pan with the spatula. 5. Flip it and cook for a further 2 minutes. 6. Serve and repeat with the rest of the mixture!

Per Serving
Calories: 487 | fat: 27g | protein: 14g | carbs: 51g | fiber: 7g | sugar: 8g | sodium: 108mg

Meditteranean Vegetable Frittata

Prep time: 10 minutes | Cook time: 25 minutes | Serves 2

1 tablespoon coconut or extra virgin olive oil
4 free range eggs
1 sweet potato, peeled and

1 peeled and sliced zucchini
2 teaspoons parsley
1 teaspoon cracked black pepper

1. Preheat broiler on a medium heat. 2. Heat the oil in a skillet under the broiler until hot. 3. Spread the potato slices across the skillet and cooking for 8 to 10 minutes or until soft. 4. Add the zucchini to the skillet and cook for a further 5 minutes. 5. Meanwhile, whisk the eggs and parsley in a separate bowl, and season with pepper before pouring mixture over the veggies in the skillet. 6. Cook for 10 minutes on a low heat until golden. 7. Remove and turn over onto a plate or serving board.

Per Serving
Calories: 214 | fat: 11g | protein: 12g | carbs: 15g | fiber: 2g | sugar: 3g | sodium: 222mg

Smoked Salmon Scrambled Eggs

Prep time: 5 minutes | Cook time: 8 minutes | Serves 4

2 tablespoons extra-virgin olive oil
6 ounces (170 g) smoked salmon, flaked

8 eggs, beaten
¼ teaspoon freshly ground black pepper

1. In a large nonstick skillet over medium-high heat, heat the olive oil until it shimmers. 2. Add the salmon and cook for 3 minutes, stirring. 3. In a medium bowl, whisk the eggs and pepper. Add them to the skillet and cook for about 5 minutes, stirring gently, until done.

Per Serving
Calories: 236 | fat: 18g | protein: 19g | carbs: 0g | fiber: 0g | sugar: 0g | sodium: 411mg

Mini Broccoli Frittatas

Prep time: 10 minutes | Cook time: 20 minutes | Serves 4

Olive oil, for greasing the muffin cups
8 eggs
¼ cup unsweetened almond milk
½ teaspoon chopped fresh basil
½ cup chopped broccoli

½ cup shredded fresh spinach
1 scallion, white and green parts, chopped
Pinch sea salt
Pinch freshly ground black pepper

1. Preheat the oven to 350ºF (180ºC). 2. Lightly oil a 6-cup muffin tin and set it aside. 3. In a medium bowl, whisk the eggs, almond milk, and basil until frothy. 4. Stir in the broccoli, spinach, and scallion. Spoon the egg mixture into the muffin cups. 5. Bake for about 20 minutes, or until the frittatas are puffed, golden, and cooked through. 6. Season with sea salt and pepper and serve.

Per Serving
Calories: 132 | fat: 9g | protein: 12g | carbs: 2g | fiber: 1g | sugar: 1g | sodium: 216mg

Wake Me Up Fruit Cereal

Prep time: 20 minutes | Cook time: 30 minutes | Serves

1 cup unsweetened pineapple, dried
½ cup warm water
1 cup cashews

½½cup coconut flakes
½ teaspoon lemon zest
1 tablespoon raw honey

1. Preheat oven to 375ºF (190ºC). 2. Soak the pineapple slices in warm water for 20 minutes until softened. 3. Combine with the rest of the ingredients and mix. 4. Spread onto a lined baking tray and bake for 20 to 30 minutes or until crispy.

Per Serving
Calories: 589 | fat: 44g | protein: 13g | carbs: 45g | fiber: 7g | sugar: 22g | sodium: 19mg

Chia Breakfast Pudding

Prep time: 5 minutes | Cook time: 0 minutes | Serves 4

¾ cup chia seeds
½ cup hemp seeds
2¼ cups coconut milk

½ cup dried cranberries
¼ cup maple syrup

1. In a medium bowl, stir together the chia seeds, hemp seeds, coconut milk, cranberries, and maple syrup, ensuring that the chia is completely mixed with the milk. 2. Cover the bowl and refrigerate overnight. 3. In the morning, stir and serve.

Per Serving
Calories: 483 | fat: 41g | protein: 9g | carbs: 25g | fiber: 6g | sugar: 17g | sodium: 22mg

Fruit-and-Seed Breakfast Bars

Prep time: 15 minutes | Cook time: 30 minutes | Serves 6

½ cup pitted dates
¾ cup toasted sunflower seeds
¾ cup toasted pumpkin seeds
¾ cup white sesame seeds

½ cup dried blueberries
½ cup dried cherries
¼ cup flaxseed
½ cup almond butter

1. Preheat the oven to 325ºF (165ºC). 2. Line an 8-by-8-inch baking dish with parchment paper. 3. In a food processor, pulse the dates until chopped into a paste. 4. Add the sunflower seeds, pumpkin seeds, sesame seeds, blueberries, cherries, and flaxseed, and pulse to combine. Scoop the mixture into a medium bowl. 5. Stir in the almond butter. Transfer the mixture to the prepared dish and press it down firmly. 6. Bake for about 30 minutes, or until firm and golden brown. 7. Cool for about 1 hour, until it is at room temperature. Remove from the baking dish and cut into 12 squares. 8. Refrigerate in a sealed container for up to 1 week.

Per Serving
Calories: 312 | fat: 22g | protein: 10g | carbs: 24g | fiber: 6g | sugar: 13g | sodium: 16mg

Maple-Tahini Oatmeal

Prep time: 5 minutes | Cook time: 15 minutes | Serves 2

2 cups water
1 cup gluten-free rolled oats
⅛ teaspoon salt

⅓ cup tahini
2 tablespoons maple syrup, divided

1. In a medium pot set over medium-high heat, stir together the water, oats, and salt. Bring to a boil. Reduce the heat to low and cover. Simmer for about 10 minutes, stirring occasionally, and checking for tenderness. 2. Stir in the tahini, letting it melt into the oatmeal. Cook for 3 to 4 minutes more, or until the oatmeal is cooked through. 3. Divide the oatmeal between two bowls. Drizzle each with 1 tablespoon of maple syrup.

Per Serving
Calories: 500 | fat: 28g | protein: 15g | carbs: 55g | fiber: 12g | sugar: 9g | sodium: 131mg

Chapter 2 Vegetarian Mains

16 **Tofu Sloppy Joes**   18
17 **Sesame-Tuna Skewers**   18
18 **Quinoa-Broccolini Sauté**   18
19 **Mushroom Egg Foo Young**   19
20 **Broccoli-Sesame Stir-Fry**   19
21 **Roasted Tri-Color Cauliflower**   19
22 **Oven-Roasted Cod with Mushrooms**   20
23 **Broccoli and Egg "Muffins"**   20
24 **Sweet Korean Lentils**   20
25 **Overstuffed Baked Sweet Potatoes**   22
26 **Whitefish Curry**   22
27 **Zucchini Spaghetti with Basil and Sweet Peas**   23
28 **Braised Bok Choy with Shiitake Mushrooms**   23

Tofu Sloppy Joes

Prep time: 10 minutes | Cook time: 15 minutes | Serves 4

2 tablespoons extra-virgin olive oil
1 onion, chopped
10 ounces (283 g) tofu, chopped
2 (14 ounces / 397 g) cans crushed tomatoes, 1 drained and 1 undrained
¼ cup apple cider vinegar
1 tablespoon chili powder
1 teaspoon garlic powder
½ teaspoon sea salt
⅛ teaspoon freshly ground black pepper

1. In a large pot over medium-high heat, heat the olive oil until it shimmers. 2. Add the onion and tofu. Cook for about 5 minutes, stirring occasionally, until the onion is soft. 3. Stir in the tomatoes, cider vinegar, chili powder, garlic powder, salt, and pepper. Simmer for 10 minutes to let the flavors blend, stirring occasionally.

Per Serving
Calories: 209 | fat: 10g | protein: 11g | carbs: 21g | fiber: 8g | sugar: 13g | sodium: 584mg

Sesame-Tuna Skewers

Prep time: 20 minutes | Cook time: 15 minutes | Serves 4 to 6

Cooking spray
¾ cup sesame seeds (mixture of black and white)
1 teaspoon salt
½ teaspoon ground ginger
¼ teaspoon freshly ground black pepper
2 tablespoons toasted sesame oil, or extra-virgin olive oil
4 (6-ounce / 170-g) thick tuna steaks, cut into 1-inch cubes

1. Preheat the oven to 400ºF (205ºC). 2. Lightly coat a rimmed baking sheet with cooking spray. 3. Soak 12 (6-inch) wooden skewers in water so they won't burn while the tuna bakes. 4. In a shallow dish, combine the sesame seeds, salt, ground ginger, and pepper. 5. In a medium bowl, toss the tuna with the sesame oil to coat. Press the oiled cubes into the sesame seed mixture. Put three cubes on each skewer. 6. Place the skewers on the prepared baking sheet and place the sheet into the preheated oven. Bake for 10 to 12 minutes, turning once halfway through.

Per Serving
Calories: 395 | fat: 22g | protein: 45g | carbs:7 g | fiber: 3g | sugar: 0g | sodium: 649mg

Quinoa-Broccolini Sauté

Prep time: 10 minutes | Cook time: 10 minutes | Serves 4

1 tablespoon coconut oil
2 leeks, white part only, sliced
2 garlic cloves, chopped
4 cups chopped broccolini
½ cup vegetable broth, or water
1 teaspoon curry powder
2 cups cooked quinoa
1 tablespoon coconut aminos

1. In a large skillet over high heat, melt the coconut oil. Add the leeks and garlic. Sauté for 2 minutes. 2. Add the broccolini and vegetable broth. Cover the pan and cook for 5 minutes. 3. Stir in the curry powder, quinoa, and coconut aminos. Cook for 2 to 3 minutes, uncovered, or until the quinoa is warmed through. 4. Serve warm as a side dish, or at room temperature as a salad.

Per Serving
Calories: 273 | fat: 6g | protein: 11g | carbs: 44g | fiber: 6g | sugar: 5g | sodium: 54mg

Mushroom Egg Foo Young

Prep time: 10 minutes | Cook time: 20 minutes | Serves 2

1 tablespoon olive oil
1 cup sliced wild mushrooms
1 teaspoon bottled minced garlic
2 cups bean sprouts
2 scallions, white and green parts, chopped
6 eggs
¼ teaspoon sea salt
1 tablespoon chopped fresh cilantro

1. Place a large skillet or wok over medium heat and add the olive oil. 2. Add the mushrooms and garlic. Sauté for about 4 minutes, or until softened. 3. Add the bean sprouts and scallions. Sauté for 5 minutes, spreading the vegetables out in the skillet. 4. In a small bowl, beat the eggs and sea salt. Pour the eggs over the vegetables in the skillet, shaking so the egg seeps through the vegetables. Cook for about 5 minutes, or until the eggs are set on the bottom. 5. Cut the omelet into quarters and flip them over. Cook the egg foo young for about 3 minutes, or until the omelet is completely cooked through. 6. Serve two pieces per person.

Per Serving

Calories: 345 | fat: 23g | protein: 28g | carbs: 12g | fiber: 1g | sugar: 2g | sodium: 511mg

Broccoli-Sesame Stir-Fry

Prep time: 10 minutes | Cook time: 10 minutes | Serves 4

2 tablespoons extra-virgin olive oil
1 teaspoon sesame oil
4 cups broccoli florets
1 tablespoon grated fresh ginger
¼ teaspoon sea salt
2 garlic cloves, minced
2 tablespoons toasted sesame seeds

1. In a large nonstick skillet over medium-high heat, heat the olive oil and sesame oil until they shimmer. 2. Add the broccoli, ginger, and salt. Cook for 5 to 7 minutes, stirring frequently, until the broccoli begins to brown. 3. Add the garlic. Cook for 30 seconds, stirring constantly. 4. Remove from the heat and stir in the sesame seeds.

Per Serving

Calories: 134 | fat: 11g | protein: 4g | carbs: 9g | fiber: 3g | sugar: 2g | sodium: 148mg

Roasted Tri-Color Cauliflower

Prep time: 10 minutes | Cook time: 20 minutes | Serves 4 to 6

1½ cups white cauliflower florets
1½ cups purple cauliflower florets
1½ cups yellow cauliflower florets
3 tablespoons extra-virgin olive oil
¼ cup fresh lemon juice
1 teaspoon salt
¼ teaspoon freshly ground black pepper

1. Preheat the oven to 400ºF (205ºC). 2. In a large bowl, combine the cauliflower, olive oil, and lemon juice. Toss to coat well. 3. Spread the cauliflower on a rimmed baking sheet and add the salt and pepper. 4. Cover with aluminum foil and bake for 15 minutes. Remove the foil and continue to bake until the cauliflower starts to brown around the edges, about 5 minutes more. 5. Serve warm or at room temperature.

Per Serving

Calories: 120 | fat: 10g | protein: 2g | carbs: 7g | fiber: 2g | sugar: 3g | sodium: 620mg

Oven-Roasted Cod with Mushrooms

Prep time: 10 minutes | Cook time: 20 minutes | Serves 4 to 6

1½ pounds (680 g) cod fillets
½ teaspoon salt, plus additional for seasoning
Freshly ground black pepper, to taste
1 tablespoon extra-virgin olive oil
1 leek, white part only, sliced thinly
8 ounces (227 g) shiitake mushrooms, stemmed, sliced
1 tablespoon coconut aminos
1 teaspoon sweet paprika
½ cup vegetable broth, or chicken broth

1. Preheat the oven to 375ºF (190ºC). 2. Season the cod with salt and pepper. Set aside. 3. In a shallow baking dish, combine the olive oil, leek, mushrooms, coconut aminos, paprika, and ½ teaspoon of salt. Season with pepper, and give everything a gentle toss to coat with the oil and spices. 4. Place the dish in the preheated oven and bake the vegetables for 10 minutes. 5. Stir the vegetables and place the cod fillets on top in a single layer. 6. Pour in the vegetable broth. Return the dish to the oven and bake for an additional 10 to 15 minutes, or until the cod is firm but cooked through.

Per Serving
Calories: 221 | fat: 6g | protein: 32g | carbs: 12g | fiber: 2g | sugar: 3g | sodium: 637mg

Broccoli and Egg "Muffins"

Prep time: 10 minutes | Cook time: 20 minutes | Serves 4

Nonstick cooking spray
2 tablespoons extra-virgin olive oil
1 onion, chopped
1 cup broccoli florets, chopped
8 eggs, beaten
1 teaspoon garlic powder
½ teaspoon sea salt
¼ teaspoon freshly ground black pepper

1. Preheat the oven to 350ºF (180ºC). 2. Spray a muffin tin with nonstick cooking spray. 3. In a large nonstick skillet over medium-high heat, heat the olive oil until it shimmers. 4. Add the onion and broccoli. Cook for 3 minutes. Spoon the vegetables evenly into 4 muffin cups. 5. In a medium bowl, beat the eggs, garlic powder, salt, and pepper. Pour them over the vegetables in the muffin cups. Bake for 15 to 17 minutes until the eggs set.

Per Serving
Calories: 207 | fat: 16g | protein: 12g | carbs: 5g | fiber: 1g | sugar: 2g | sodium: 366mg

Sweet Korean Lentils

Prep time: 15 minutes | Cook time: 20 minutes | Serves 4

1 tablespoon avocado oil
1 small white onion, diced
2 garlic cloves, minced
2 cups vegetable broth
1 cup dried lentils, sorted and rinsed
3 tablespoons coconut aminos
2 tablespoons coconut sugar
1 tablespoon rice vinegar
1 teaspoon sesame oil
½ teaspoon ground ginger
¼ teaspoon red pepper flakes
1 tablespoon sesame seeds (optional)
2 scallions, sliced (optional)

1. To a stockpot over medium heat, add the avocado oil, onion, and garlic. Sauté for 5 minutes, or until the onion is translucent. 2. Stir in the broth, lentils, coconut aminos, coconut sugar, vinegar, sesame oil, ginger, and red pepper flakes. Increase the heat to medium-high and bring to a simmer. Reduce the heat to low, cover, and cook for 15 minutes, or until the lentils are cooked. 3. Garnish with the sesame seeds and scallions (if using).

Per Serving
Calories: 281 | fat: 5g | protein: 14g | carbs: 45g | fiber: 10g | sugar: 7g | sodium: 294mg

Chapter 2: Vegetarian Mains | 21

Overstuffed Baked Sweet Potatoes

Prep time: 15 minutes | Cook time: 25 minutes | Serves 4

4 medium sweet potatoes
1 tablespoon avocado oil
1 small white onion, thinly sliced
2 garlic cloves, minced
1 (14-ounce / 397-g) can black beans, drained and rinsed well
12 cherry tomatoes, chopped
½ teaspoon chili powder
¼ teaspoon red pepper flakes
¼ teaspoon salt
1 large avocado, sliced
Juice of 1 lime

1. Preheat the oven to 400°F (205°C). 2. With a fork, poke holes 5 to 6 times into each sweet potato. Loosely wrap each sweet potato in aluminum foil, place them on a baking sheet, and bake for 25 minutes, or until cooked. 3. Meanwhile, in a large skillet or sauté pan over medium heat, heat the avocado oil. Add the onion and garlic, and sauté for 5 minutes. 4. Stir in the beans, tomatoes, chili powder, red pepper flakes, and salt. Cook for about 7 minutes. Remove from the heat. 5. When the sweet potatoes are cooked, remove them from the oven and carefully unwrap the foil. Slice each potato lengthwise, almost through to the bottom. Open the potatoes to create room for the filling, and spoon equal amounts of filling into each. 6. Top with avocado slices and a drizzle of lime juice.

Per Serving
Calories: 326 | fat: 10g | protein: 10g | carbs: 51g | fiber: 13g | sugar: 9g | sodium: 236mg

Whitefish Curry

Prep time: 15 minutes | Cook time: 15 minutes | Serves 4 to 6

2 tablespoons coconut oil
1 onion, chopped
2 garlic cloves, minced
1 tablespoon minced fresh ginger
2 teaspoons curry powder
1 teaspoon salt
¼ teaspoon freshly ground black pepper
1 (4-inch) piece lemongrass (white part only), bruised with the back of a knife
2 cups cubed butternut squash
2 cups chopped broccoli
1 (13½-ounce / 383-g) can coconut milk
1 cup vegetable broth, or chicken broth
1 pound (454 g) firm whitefish fillets
¼ cup chopped fresh cilantro
1 scallion, sliced thinly
Lemon wedges, for garnish

1. In a large pot over medium-high heat, melt the coconut oil. Add the onion, garlic, ginger, curry powder, salt, and pepper. Sauté for 5 minutes. 2. Add the lemongrass, butternut squash, and broccoli. Sauté for 2 minutes more. 3. Stir in the coconut milk and vegetable broth and bring to a boil. Reduce the heat to simmer and add the fish. Cover the pot and simmer for 5 minutes, or until the fish is cooked through. Remove and discard the lemongrass. 4. Ladle the curry into a serving bowl. Garnish with the cilantro and scallion and serve with the lemon wedges.

Per Serving
Calories: 553 | fat: 39g | protein: 34g | carbs: 22g | fiber: 6g | sugar: 7g | sodium: 881mg

Zucchini Spaghetti with Basil and Sweet Peas

Prep time: 15 minutes | Cook time: 0 minutes | Serves 4

1 cup packed fresh basil leaves, plus more for garnish
1 cup packed fresh oregano leaves
½ cup almonds
2 teaspoons bottled minced garlic
Juice of 1 lemon (or 3 tablespoons)
Zest of 1 lemon (optional)
Pinch sea salt
Pinch freshly ground black pepper
¼ cup olive oil
2 large green zucchini, julienned or spiralized
1 cup peas (fresh or frozen and thawed)

1. In a food processor, combine the basil, oregano, almonds, garlic, lemon juice, lemon zest (if using), sea salt, and pepper. Pulse until very finely chopped. 2. While the processor is running, add the olive oil in a thin stream until a thick paste forms. 3. In a bowl, combine the zucchini noodles and peas. Add the pesto, 1 tablespoon at a time, until you have the desired flavor. Serve immediately, garnished with basil leaves. 4. Refrigerate any leftover pesto in a sealed container for up to 2 weeks.

Per Serving
Calories: 280 | fat: 21g | protein: 8g | carbs: 23g | fiber: 12g | sugar: 4g | sodium: 14mg

Braised Bok Choy with Shiitake Mushrooms

Prep time: 10 minutes | Cook time: 10 minutes | Serves 4

1 tablespoon coconut oil
8 baby bok choy, halved lengthwise
½ cup water
1 tablespoon coconut aminos
1 cup shiitake mushrooms, stemmed, sliced thinly
Salt, to taste
Freshly ground black pepper, to taste
1 scallion, sliced thinly
1 tablespoon toasted sesame seeds

1. In a large pan over high heat, melt the coconut oil. Add the bok choy in a single layer. 2. Add the water, coconut aminos, and mushrooms to the pan. Cover and braise the vegetables for 5 to 10 minutes, or until the bok choy is tender. 3. Remove the pan from the heat. Season the vegetables with salt and pepper. 4. Transfer the bok choy and mushrooms to a serving dish and garnish with the scallions and sesame seeds.

Per Serving
Calories: 285 | fat: 8g | protein: 26g | carbs: 43g | fiber: 18g | sugar: 21g | sodium: 1035mg

Chapter 3 Vegetables and Sides

29 Slow-Roasted Sweet Potatoes   26
30 Kale-Stuffed Mushrooms   26
31 Caramelized Celeriac   26
32 Homemade Avocado Sushi   28
33 Rustic Garlic and Chive Quinoa   28
34 Cauliflower Purée   28
35 Blanched Green Veggies with Radishes   29
36 Rosemary Wild Rice   29
37 Crispy Oven-Roasted Broccoli with Italian Spice Trio   29
38 Lime-Chili Roasted Cauliflower   31
39 Simple Spaghetti Squash   31
40 Savory Flax Waffles   31
41 Zainy Zucchini Ketchup   32
42 Roasted Butternut Squash Mash   32

Slow-Roasted Sweet Potatoes

Prep time: 10 minutes | Cook time: 40 minutes | Serves 4

Olive oil, for greasing the baking dish
3 sweet potatoes, peeled and cut into large chunks
1 tablespoon pure maple syrup
½ teaspoon ground allspice
½ teaspoon ground ginger
¼ teaspoon ground nutmeg
Pinch sea salt
½ cup unsweetened apple juice

1. Preheat the oven to 350°F (180°C). 2. Lightly grease an 8-by-8-inch baking dish with olive oil. 3. In a large bowl, toss the sweet potatoes, maple syrup, all-spice, ginger, nutmeg, and sea salt until well mixed. Transfer the sweet potatoes to the prepared dish, and pour in the apple juice. 4. Cover the dish and bake the potatoes for about 40 minutes, or until very tender.

Per Serving
Calories: 295 | fat: 1g | protein: 4g | carbs: 70g | fiber: 9g | sugar: 10g | sodium: 56mg

Kale-Stuffed Mushrooms

Prep time: 15 minutes | Cook time: 28 minutes | Serves 4

16 large white button mushrooms, stemmed
2 teaspoons olive oil
½ cup finely chopped sweet onion
1 teaspoon bottled minced garlic
2 cups finely shredded kale
1 cup chopped water-packed canned artichoke hearts
1 teaspoon chopped fresh basil
1 teaspoon chopped fresh oregano
⅛ teaspoon sea salt

1. Preheat the oven to 375°F (190°C). 2. Arrange the mushroom caps, hollow-side up, on a baking sheet. 3. Place a large skillet over medium-high heat and add the olive oil. 4. Add the onion and garlic. Sauté for about 3 minutes, or until tender. 5. Stir in the kale, artichoke hearts, basil, oregano, and sea salt. Sauté for about 5 minutes, or until the kale is wilted. 6. With the back of a spoon, squeeze the liquid out of the filling into the skillet and evenly divide the mixture among the mushroom caps. 7. Bake for about 20 minutes, or until the mushrooms are tender. Serve warm.

Per Serving
Calories: 75 | fat: 3g | protein: 5g | carbs: 11g | fiber: 3g | sugar: 2g | sodium: 242mg

Caramelized Celeriac

Prep time: 10 minutes | Cook time: 20 minutes | Serves 4

2 celeriac, peeled and diced
1 tablespoon olive oil
½ teaspoon ground nutmeg
½ teaspoon ground cinnamon
⅛ teaspoon sea salt
2 tablespoons pure maple syrup
1 teaspoon freshly squeezed lemon juice

1. Preheat the oven to 400°F (205°C). 2. Line a rimmed baking sheet with aluminum foil. 3. In a large bowl, toss together the celeriac, olive oil, nutmeg, cinnamon, and sea salt. 4. Spread the celeriac on the prepared sheet and roast for 15 to 20 minutes, or until very tender and lightly caramelized. 5. Transfer the celeriac to a serving bowl. Add the maple syrup and lemon juice. Toss to coat and then serve.

Per Serving
Calories: 157 | fat: 4g | protein: 4g | carbs: 29g | fiber: 4g | sugar: 6g | sodium: 79mg

Chapter 3: Vegetables and Sides | 27

Homemade Avocado Sushi

Prep time: 20 minutes | Cook time: 15 minutes | Serves 4

1½ cups dry quinoa
3 cups water, plus additional for rolling
½ teaspoon salt
6 nori sheets
3 avocados, halved, pitted, and sliced thinly, divided

1 small cucumber, halved, seeded, and cut into matchsticks, divided
Coconut aminos, for dipping (optional)

1. Rinse the quinoa in a fine-mesh sieve. 2. In a medium pot set over high heat, combine the rinsed quinoa, water, and salt. Bring to a boil. Reduce the heat to low. Cover and simmer for 15 minutes. Fluff the quinoa with a fork. 3. On a cutting board, lay out 1 nori sheet. Spread ½ cup of quinoa over the sheet, leaving 2 to 3 inches uncovered at the top. 4. Place 5 or 6 avocado slices across the bottom of the nori sheet (the side closest to you) in a row. Add 5 or 6 cucumber matchsticks on top. 5. Starting at the bottom, tightly roll up the nori sheet. sheet. Dab the uncovered top with water to seal the roll. 6. Slice the sushi roll into 6 pieces. 7. Repeat with the remaining 5 nori sheets, quinoa, and vegetables. 8. Serve with the coconut aminos (if using).

Per Serving
Calories: 557 | fat: 33g | protein: 13g | carbs: 57g | fiber: 15g | sugar: 2g | sodium: 309mg

Rustic Garlic and Chive Quinoa

Prep time: 10 minutes | Cook time: 30 minutes | Serves 2

½ cup of kidney beans
½ cup of uncooked quinoa
2 cups of low-salt vegetable broth
3 green onion stalks, diced

4 cloves of garlic, minced
¼ teaspoon of black pepper
1 tablespoon extra virgin olive oil

1. Sauté garlic and onion in olive oil, in a large pan at medium heat until onions soften. 2. Lower heat. Add the quinoa, kidney beans and vegetable broth. 3. Cover the pan and simmer for around 15 to 20 minutes or until quinoa is soft and liquid is absorbed. 4. Serve with the diced green onion scattered over the quinoa and a little black pepper to taste.

Per Serving
Calories: 495 | fat: 13g | protein: 23g | carbs: 74g | fiber: 12g | sugar: 7g | sodium: 566mg

Cauliflower Purée

Prep time: 15 minutes | Cook time: 10 minutes | Serves 4

1 head cauliflower, broken into florets
1 garlic clove
2 teaspoons salt, divided

¼ teaspoon freshly ground black pepper
½ cup coconut milk
1 tablespoon extra-virgin olive oil

1. Bring a large pot of water to a boil over high heat. Add the cauliflower, garlic clove, and 1 teaspoon of salt. Boil for about 5 minutes, or until the cauliflower is tender. 2. Drain the cauliflower with the garlic clove and transfer to a large bowl. Mash with a potato masher. 3. Add the remaining 1 teaspoon of salt, the pepper, and coconut milk to the mash. Stir until well combined. 4. Place the purée in a serving bowl and drizzle with olive oil.

Per Serving
Calories: 117 | fat: 11g | protein: 2g | carbs: 6g | fiber: 2g | sugar: 3g | sodium: 1087mg

Blanched Green Veggies with Radishes

Prep time: 15 minutes | Cook time: 5 minutes | Serves 4

1½ tablespoons olive oil
1 pound (454 g) asparagus spears, woody ends trimmed
½ pound (227 g) green beans, trimmed
1 cup fava beans (fresh or frozen and thawed)
1 cup peas (fresh or frozen and thawed)
½ cup whole radishes, trimmed
1 tablespoon rice vinegar
Sea salt, to taste
Freshly ground black pepper, to taste

1. Place a large skillet over medium heat and add the olive oil. 2. Add the asparagus, green beans, fava beans, and peas. Sauté for about 5 minutes, or until crisp-tender. 3. Add the radishes and rice vinegar, or and toss to combine. 4. Season the veggies with sea salt and pepper and serve.

Per Serving
Calories: 247 | fat: 6g | protein: 15g | carbs: 35g | fiber: 16g | sugar: 5g | sodium: 17mg

Rosemary Wild Rice

Prep time: 10 minutes | Cook time: 45 minutes | Serves 4

1 cup wild rice
3½ cups vegetable broth
1 tablespoon extra-virgin olive oil
1 teaspoon salt
¼ teaspoon freshly ground black pepper
1 teaspoon chopped fresh rosemary (optional)

1. Rinse the wild rice in a fine-mesh strainer and drain well. Transfer to a medium pot. 2. Add the broth, olive oil, salt, and pepper. 3. Bring to a boil over a high heat, then reduce to a simmer. Partially cover the pot to allow steam to escape and cook for 35 to 45 minutes. The rice is done when some of the strands break open. 4. Drain any additional liquid, then add the rosemary (if using), fluff the rice with a fork, and serve.

Per Serving
Calories: 190 | fat: 4g | protein: 6g | carbs: 33g | fiber: 3g | sugar: 2g | sodium: 710mg

Crispy Oven-Roasted Broccoli with Italian Spice Trio

Prep time: 15 minutes | Cook time: 20 minutes | Serves 4

Italian Spice Trio:
2 tablespoons dried oregano
2 tablespoons fennel seeds
½ teaspoon crushed red pepper flakes
1 large or 2 small heads broccoli, cut into 1-inch florets
¼ cup extra-virgin olive oil
1 teaspoon kosher salt
¼ teaspoon freshly ground black pepper
Zest and juice of 1 lemon

Make the spice trio:
1. Combine the oregano, fennel seeds, and red pepper flakes in an airtight container. Store at room temperature for up to 1 month. 2. Place two racks in the lower third of the oven and preheat the oven to 450ºF (235ºC). Use the convection setting if available. Combine the broccoli, olive oil, 1 tablespoon of the spice trio, salt, pepper, and lemon zest in a large bowl. Stir to coat the broccoli evenly. Spread the broccoli evenly on two baking sheets. Roast for 10 minutes. 3. Remove from the oven and stir. Place the sheets on opposite racks and roast until the broccoli has caramelized and is just cooked through, 5 to 10 minutes. Stir in 1 teaspoon lemon juice, adding more to taste. Serve hot or at room temperature.

Per Serving
Calories: 120 | fat: 7g | protein: 5g | carbs: 13g | fiber: 6g | sugar: 3g | sodium: 324mg

Lime-Chili Roasted Cauliflower

Prep time: 10 minutes | Cook time: 15 minutes | Serves 4

1½ teaspoons ground cumin
1 teaspoon salt
½ teaspoon chili powder
½ teaspoon freshly ground black pepper
½ teaspoon garlic powder
1 head cauliflower, roughly chopped into bite-size pieces
3 tablespoons freshly squeezed lime juice
3 tablespoons ghee, melted

1. Preheat the oven to 450ºF (235ºC). 2. In a small bowl, mix the cumin, salt, chili powder, pepper, and garlic powder. 3. Spread the cauliflower in a baking pan. Drizzle with the lime juice and ghee. Sprinkle with the spice mixture and toss to coat. 4. Bake for 15 minutes.

Per Serving
Calories: 138 | fat: 11g | protein: 3g | carbs: 9g | fiber: 3g | sugar: 2g | sodium: 613mg

Simple Spaghetti Squash

Prep time: 15 minutes | Cook time: 8 hours | Serves 4 to 6

1 spaghetti squash, washed well
2 cups water

1. Using a fork, poke 10 to 15 holes all around the outside of the spaghetti squash. Put the squash and the water in your slow cooker. 2. Cover the cooker and set to low. Cook for 8 hours. 3. Transfer the squash from the slow cooker to a cutting board. Let sit for 15 minutes to cool. 4. Halve the squash lengthwise. Using a spoon, scrape the seeds out of the center of the squash. Then, using a fork, scrape at the flesh until it shreds into a spaghetti-like texture. Serve warm.

Per Serving
Calories: 60 | fat: 0g | protein: 0g | carbs: 15g | fiber: 0g | sugar: 0g | sodium: 42mg

Savory Flax Waffles

Prep time: 5 minutes | Cook time: 20 minutes | Makes 4 waffles

4 large eggs
¼ cup coconut cream
1 tablespoon coconut vinegar
1 cup flaxseed meal
½ teaspoon fine Himalayan salt
½ teaspoon garlic powder
½ teaspoon ground black pepper
½ teaspoon onion powder

1. In a large bowl, whisk together the eggs, coconut cream, and vinegar until well combined. Add the flaxseed meal, salt, garlic powder, pepper, and onion powder and mix until a thick batter forms. 2. Preheat a waffle iron per the manufacturer's instructions. When it's ready, pour in about ¼ cup of the batter. Cook until crispy, about 5 minutes, depending on your appliance. Repeat with the remaining batter. 3. Serve immediately. Store leftovers in an airtight container in the fridge for up to 1 week. To reheat, toast in a preheated 400ºF (205ºC) oven for 4 minutes.

Per Serving
Calories: 249 | fat: 19g | protein: 12g | carbs: 9g | fiber: 8g | sugar: 1g | sodium: 260mg

Zainy Zucchini Ketchup

Prep time: 15 minutes | Cook time: 0 minutes | Serves 4

2 zucchinis, peeled and sliced
2½ cup fresh parsley
2 tablespoons lemon juice
1 tablespoon extra virgin olive oil
1 garlic clove, minced
A pinch of black pepper
2 tablespoons chopped walnuts

1. Allow zucchini to dry out a little by slicing and placing on kitchen towel to soak up the moisture for 10 minutes or longer if possible. 2. Process the zucchini with the rest of the ingredients (apart from the nuts) until smooth. 3. Fold in the nuts to the mixture and then refrigerate for at least 10 minutes and serve.

Per Serving
Calories: 71 | fat: 6g | protein: 2g | carbs: 4g | fiber: 2g | sugar: 1g | sodium: 22mg

Roasted Butternut Squash Mash

Prep time: 10 minutes | Cook time: 30 minutes | Serves 4

3 cups cubed butternut squash
1 cup coarsely chopped carrot
1 large green apple, peeled, cored, and chopped
3 tablespoons extra-virgin olive oil
1 teaspoon salt
¼ teaspoon freshly ground black pepper
½ cup unsweetened almond milk

1. Preheat the oven to 375ºF (190ºC). 2. Combine the squash, carrot, and apple in a large bowl. Add the oil, salt, and pepper and toss to mix well. 3. Transfer the vegetables to a rimmed baking sheet and roast until the vegetables are tender and lightly browned, 20 to 30 minutes. 4. Return the vegetables to the bowl. 5. Using a potato masher, mash the vegetables, then add the milk and stir until mostly smooth. (The mixture will be slightly lumpy.) Serve immediately.

Per Serving
Calories: 170 | fat: 11g | protein: 2g | carbs: 20g | fiber: 4g | sugar: 7g | sodium: 630mg

Chapter 4 Beef, Pork, and Lamb

43 **Thai Beef with Coconut Milk**   35

44 **Pork Tenderloin with Dijon-Cider Glaze**   35

45 **Beef and Bell Pepper Fajitas**   35

46 **Rosemary Lamb Chops**   36

47 **Chocolate Chili**   36

48 **Grainy Mustard-Crusted Lamb**   36

49 **Thin-Cut Pork Chops with Mustardy Kale**   37

50 **Berry Bliss Slow Cooker Pork**   37

51 **Hearty Bolognese**   38

52 **Herbed Lamb-Zucchini Boats**   38

53 **Chili-Lime Pork Loin**   38

54 **Slow Cooker Shawarma**   40

55 **Garlicky Lamb Stew**   40

56 **Pork Sausage**   41

57 **Sesame-Ginger Bok Choy and Beef Stir-Fry**   41

Thai Beef with Coconut Milk

Prep time: 10 minutes | Cook time: 30 minutes | Serves 2

2 tablespoons coconut oil
1 teaspoon crushed garlic
1 onion cut into wedges
8 ounces (227 g) round steak, cut into strips
2 cups cubed potatoes
1 lime
2 cups cubed Carrots
1 cup coconut milk
½ cup beef stock
Black pepper to taste

1. Heat the wok over a medium heat, and then add in the oil, garlic, and the onion, cooking for 1 minute. 2. Put the beef into the wok and cook for 3 minutes. 3. Add in the potatoes, Carrots into the wok and stir-fry for 4 minutes. 4. Add the coconut milk, beef stock, and black pepper and allow to simmer for 20 to 25 minutes or until beef is cooked through. 5. Serve hot with your choice of greens and a wedge of lime to squeeze!

Per Serving
Calories: 563 | fat: 45g | protein: 30g | carbs: 15g | fiber: 3g | sugar: 4g | sodium: 235mg

Pork Tenderloin with Dijon-Cider Glaze

Prep time: 5 minutes | Cook time: 25 minutes | Serves 4

¼ cup apple cider vinegar
¼ cup coconut sugar
3 tablespoons Dijon mustard
2 teaspoons garlic powder
Dash salt
1 (1½-pound / 680-g) pork tenderloin

1. In a small bowl, stir together the vinegar, coconut sugar, mustard, garlic powder, and salt until the sugar dissolves. Brush this mixture over the pork loin. 2. Place a grill pan over medium-high heat and add the pork. Sear for 2 minutes per side. 3. Spoon half of the vinegar mixture over the pork and reduce the heat to medium. Cover the pan and cook for 10 minutes. 4. Spoon the remaining vinegar mixture over the pork. Cook for 5 minutes, or until the center of the pork reaches 145ºF (63ºC). Transfer the pork to a plate. 5. Bring the vinegar mixture remaining in the pan to a simmer. Cook for 5 minutes to reduce and thicken. 6. Serve the pork drizzled with the glaze.

Per Serving
Calories: 268 | fat: 6g | protein: 36g | carbs: 16g | fiber: 0g | sugar: 7g | sodium: 260mg

Beef and Bell Pepper Fajitas

Prep time: 5 minutes | Cook time: 10 minutes | Serves 4

3 tablespoons extra-virgin olive oil
1½ pounds (680 g) flank steak, cut against the grain into ½-inch strips
2 green bell peppers, sliced
1 onion, sliced
1 cup store-bought salsa
1 teaspoon garlic powder
½ teaspoon sea salt

1. In a large nonstick skillet over medium-high heat, heat the olive oil until it shimmers. 2. Add the beef, bell peppers, and onion. Cook for about 6 minutes, stirring occasionally, until the beef browns. 3. Stir in the salsa, garlic powder, and salt. Cook for 3 minutes, stirring.

Per Serving
Calories: 470 | fat: 25g | protein:49 g | carbs: 12g | fiber: 3g | sugar: 6g | sodium: 562mg

Rosemary Lamb Chops

Prep time: 15 minutes | Cook time: 7 to 8 hours | Serves 4 to 6

1 medium onion, sliced
2 teaspoons garlic powder
2 teaspoons dried rosemary
1 teaspoon sea salt
½ teaspoon dried thyme leaves
Freshly ground black pepper, to taste
8 bone-in lamb chops (about 3 pounds / 1.4 kg)
2 tablespoons balsamic vinegar

1. Line the bottom of the slow cooker with the onion slices. 2. In a small bowl, stir together the garlic powder, rosemary, salt, thyme, and pepper. Rub the chops evenly with the spice mixture, and gently place them in the slow cooker. 3. Drizzle the vinegar over the top. 4. Cover the cooker and set to low. Cook for 7 to 8 hours and serve.

Per Serving

Calories: 327 | fat: 14g | protein: 43g | carbs: 4g | fiber: 1g | sugar: 1g | sodium: 1070mg

Chocolate Chili

Prep time: 15 minutes | Cook time: 45 minutes | Serves 4 to 6

1 tablespoon extra-virgin olive oil
1 pound (454 g) lean ground beef
1 large onion, chopped
2 garlic cloves, minced
1 tablespoon unsweetened cocoa
1½ teaspoons chili powder
1 teaspoon salt
½ teaspoon ground cumin
2 cups chicken broth
1 cup tomato sauce

1. In a Dutch oven, heat the oil over high heat. Add the ground beef and brown well, about 5 minutes. 2. Add the onion, garlic, cocoa, chili powder, salt, and cumin and cook, stirring, for an additional minute. 3. Add the chicken broth and tomato sauce and bring to a boil. Reduce the heat to a simmer, cover, and cook, stirring occasionally, for 30 to 40 minutes. If the sauce becomes too thick as it cooks, add more chicken broth or water to thin it. 4. Ladle into bowls and serve.

Per Serving

Calories: 370 | fat: 27g | protein: 23g | carbs: 9g | fiber: 2g | sugar: 4g | sodium: 1010mg

Grainy Mustard-Crusted Lamb

Prep time: 10 minutes | Cook time: 35 minutes | Serves 4

¼ cup whole-grain Dijon mustard
2 tablespoons chopped fresh thyme
1 tablespoon chopped fresh rosemary
2 (8-rib) frenched lamb racks, patted dry
Sea salt, to taste
Freshly ground black pepper, to taste
1 tablespoon olive oil

1. Preheat the oven to 425ºF (220ºC). 2. In a small bowl, stir together the mustard, thyme, and rosemary. 3. Lightly season the lamb racks with sea salt and pepper. 4. Place a large ovenproof skillet over medium-high heat and add the olive oil. 5. Add the lamb racks. Pan-sear for about 2 minutes per side, turning once. Remove the skillet from the heat. 6. Turn the racks upright in the skillet with the bones interlaced, and spread the mustard mixture over the outside surface of the lamb. Roast for about 30 minutes for medium, or until your desired doneness. 7. Remove the lamb racks from the oven and let them rest for 10 minutes. Cut the racks into chops and serve 4 per person.

Per Serving

Calories: 469 | fat: 21g | protein: 65g | carbs: 2g | fiber: 1g | sugar: 0g | sodium: 211mg

Thin-Cut Pork Chops with Mustardy Kale

Prep time: 10 minutes | Cook time: 15 minutes | Serves 4

4 thin-cut pork chops

1 teaspoon sea salt, divided

¼ teaspoon freshly ground black pepper, divided

4 tablespoons Dijon mustard, divided

3 tablespoons extra-virgin olive oil

½ red onion, finely chopped

4 cups stemmed and chopped kale

2 tablespoons apple cider vinegar

1. Preheat the oven to 425ºF (220ºC). 2. Season the pork chops with ½ teaspoon of the salt and ⅛ teaspoon of the pepper. Spread 2 tablespoons of the mustard over them and put them on a rimmed baking sheet. Bake for about 15 minutes, or until the pork registers an internal temperature of 165ºF (74ºC) on an instant-read meat thermometer. 3. While the pork cooks, in a large nonstick skillet over medium-high, heat the olive oil until it shimmers. 4. Add the red onion and kale. Cook for about 7 minutes, stirring occasionally, until the vegetables soften. 5. In a small bowl, whisk the remaining 2 tablespoons of mustard, the cider vinegar, the remaining ½ teaspoon of salt, and the remaining ⅛ teaspoon of pepper. Add this to the kale. Cook for 2 minutes, stirring.

Per Serving

Calories: 504 | fat: 39g | protein: 28g | carbs: 10g | fiber: 2g | sugar: 0g | sodium: 595mg

Berry Bliss Slow Cooker Pork

Prep time: 10 minutes | Cook time: 6 hours | Serves 4

4 thick-cut boneless pork chops

1 teaspoon fine Himalayan salt

½ teaspoon ground black pepper

2 tablespoons avocado oil

2 cups raspberries or blackberries

½ cup bone broth

½ cup chopped red onions

¼ cup chopped fresh parsley

¼ cup red wine vinegar

1 teaspoon peeled and minced fresh ginger

Pinch of ground nutmeg

Dash of ground cinnamon

10 drops liquid stevia (optional)

1. Heat a large skillet over medium heat, or heat an electric pressure cooker on sauté mode. Sprinkle the pork chops with the salt and pepper. When the skillet or pressure cooker is hot, pour in the oil and sear the chops for 3 minutes on each side. 2. Place the seared pork chops in the slow cooker so they are all lying flat. Add the remaining ingredients. Cover and cook on low for 6 hours. 3. Remove the lid from the slow cooker and use tongs to carefully remove the pork chops. Serve with the tender berries and sauce spooned on top of the chops. It's quite lovely. 4. Store leftovers in an airtight container in the fridge for up to 4 days. Reheat in a covered skillet over medium heat for 5 to 10 minutes.

Per Serving

Calories: 432 | fat: 14g | protein: 44g | carbs: 32g | fiber: 5g | sugar: 26g | sodium: 545mg

Hearty Bolognese

Prep time: 15 minutes | Cook time: 7 to 8 hours | Serves 4 to 6

1 tablespoon extra-virgin olive oil
3 garlic cloves, minced
½ cup chopped onion
⅔ cup chopped celery
⅔ cup chopped carrot
1 pound (454 g) ground beef
1 (14-ounce / 397-g) can diced tomatoes
1 tablespoon white wine vinegar
⅛ teaspoon ground nutmeg
2 bay leaves
½ teaspoon red pepper flakes
Dash sea salt
Dash freshly ground black pepper

1. Coat the bottom of the slow cooker with the olive oil. 2. Add the garlic, onion, celery, carrot, ground beef, tomatoes, vinegar, nutmeg, bay leaves, red pepper flakes, salt, and black pepper. Using a fork, break up the ground beef as much as possible. 3. Cover the cooker and set to low. Cook for 7 to 8 hours. 4. Remove and discard the bay leaves. Stir, breaking up the meat completely, and serve.

Per Serving
Calories: 314 | fat: 21g | protein: 22g | carbs: 10g | fiber: 2g | sugar: 5g | sodium: 376mg

Herbed Lamb-Zucchini Boats

Prep time: 15 minutes | Cook time: 40 minutes | Serves 6

6 zucchini, ends trimmed, halved lengthwise
1 onion, finely diced
2 tablespoons water
1 pound (454 g) ground lamb
1 to 2 tablespoons fresh rosemary, minced
½ teaspoon salt

1. Preheat the oven to 350ºF (180ºC). 2. Line a baking sheet with parchment paper. 3. With a small spoon, gently hollow out about 1 inch of space along the length of the inside of the zucchini halves. 4. In a large pan set over medium heat, sauté the onion in the water for about 5 minutes, or until soft. 5. Add the ground lamb, rosemary, and salt. Cook for 10 minutes, breaking up the lamb with a spoon. Remove from the heat. 6. Place the zucchini on the prepared sheet, hollow-side up. 7. Fill each zucchini with equal amounts of the lamb mixture. 8. Place the sheet in the preheated oven and bake for 25 minutes, or until the lamb is fully cooked and the zucchini are tender.

Per Serving
Calories: 183 | fat: 6g | protein: 24g | carbs: 9g | fiber: 3g | sugar: 4g | sodium: 272mg

Chili-Lime Pork Loin

Prep time: 15 minutes | Cook time: 6 to 7 hours | Serves 4 to 6

3 teaspoons chili powder
2 teaspoons garlic powder
1 teaspoon ground cumin
½ teaspoon sea salt
2 (1-pound / 454-g) pork tenderloins
1 cup broth of choice
¼ cup freshly squeezed lime juice

1. In a small bowl, stir together the chili powder, garlic powder, cumin, and salt. Rub the pork all over with the spice mixture, and put it in the slow cooker. 2. Pour the broth and lime juice around the pork in the cooker. 3. Cover the cooker and set to low. Cook for 6 to 7 hours. 4. Remove the pork from the slow cooker and let rest for 5 minutes. Slice the pork against the grain into medallions before serving.

Per Serving
Calories: 259 | fat: 5g | protein: 50g | carbs: 5g | fiber: 1g | sugar: 0g | sodium: 510mg

Slow Cooker Shawarma

Prep time: 10 minutes | Cook time: 8 hours | Serves 6

1 tablespoon fine Himalayan salt
1 tablespoon ground black pepper
1 tablespoon ground cumin
1 teaspoon ground cardamom
½ teaspoon ground nutmeg
3 pounds (1.4 kg) boneless chuck short rib or shoulder
¼ cup coconut vinegar or red wine vinegar
3 tablespoons avocado oil
5 cloves garlic, peeled
1 large onion, quartered
1 lemon, quartered
1 navel orange, quartered

1. In a small bowl, mix together the salt, pepper, cumin, cardamom, and nutmeg. Rub the spice mixture all over the meat. 2. Place the meat in a large bowl and drizzle the vinegar and oil all over it. Add the garlic, onion, and citrus. Toss to combine, squeezing some juice out of the fruit. Cover and set in the refrigerator to marinate overnight. 3. When you're ready to cook, put everything in the slow cooker, meat on the bottom, citrus and onion quarters on top. Cook on low for 8 hours. 4. Discard the large pieces of citrus. Use two forks to shred the beef. If you like crispy beef, you can spread it on a sheet pan and broil it for 5 minutes to get delicious crispy tips. Divide the shredded beef among five or six plates, spoon the delicious slow cooker sauce over the meat, and serve. 5. Store leftovers in an airtight container in the fridge for up to 5 days or in the freezer for up to 30 days. To thaw and reheat, place in a preheated 400ºF (205ºC) oven for 10 to 20 minutes.

Per Serving
Calories: 496 | fat: 28g | protein: 54g | carbs: 8g | fiber: 2g | sugar: 2g | sodium: 600mg

Garlicky Lamb Stew

Prep time: 15 minutes | Cook time: 15 minutes | Serves 4

1 pound (454 g) ground lamb
1 tablespoon extra-virgin olive oil
1 onion, chopped
1 teaspoon dried oregano
½ teaspoon sea salt
¼ teaspoon freshly ground black pepper
1 (28 ounces / 794 g) can chopped tomatoes, drained
5 garlic cloves, minced

1. In a large nonstick skillet over medium-high heat, cook the lamb for about 5 minutes, crumbling it with a wooden spoon until it browns. Drain the fat and remove the lamb to a dish. 2. Return the skillet to the heat, add the olive oil, and heat it until it shimmers. 3. Add the onion, oregano, salt, and pepper. Cook for 5 minutes, stirring, until the onions are soft. 4. Return the lamb to the skillet and stir in the tomatoes. Cook for 3 minutes, stirring occasionally, or until heated through. 5. Add the garlic. Cook for 30 seconds, stirring constantly.

Per Serving
Calories: 295 | fat: 12g | protein: 34g | carbs: 12g | fiber: 3g | sugar: 7g | sodium: 332mg

Pork Sausage

Prep time: 10 minutes | Cook time: 15 minutes | Makes 10 patties

2 pounds (907 g) ground pork
2 ribs celery, minced
4 cloves garlic, minced
2 teaspoons Dijon mustard
2 teaspoons fine Himalayan salt

1 teaspoon dried thyme leaves
1 teaspoon ground black pepper
¼ teaspoon ginger powder
¼ teaspoon ground cinnamon
Pinch of ground nutmeg

1. Place all of the ingredients in a large bowl and mix thoroughly with your hands. 2. Heat a large cast-iron skillet over medium heat. While it heats, shape the pork mixture into patties, about ¼ cup per patty. 3. When the skillet is hot, place four or five patties in the pan, without crowding the pan. Cook the patties for 6 minutes per side, or until the internal temperature reaches 165ºF (74ºC). Repeat with the remaining patties. 4. This sausage stores well side by side in an airtight container in the refrigerator for up to 5 days or in the freezer for up to 30 days. To reheat, place in a preheated 350ºF (180ºC) oven for 8 to 10 minutes.

Per Serving

Calories: 157 | fat: 12g | protein: 9g | carbs: 2g | fiber: 0g | sugar: 0g | sodium: 364mg

Sesame-Ginger Bok Choy and Beef Stir-Fry

Prep time: 15 minutes | Cook time: 10 minutes | Serves 4

12 ounces (340 g) flank steak, cut into thin 2-inch strips
½ teaspoon salt
¼ teaspoon freshly ground black pepper
2 teaspoons avocado oil
1 tablespoon sesame oil
2 garlic cloves, minced

4 heads baby bok choy, quartered lengthwise
3 tablespoons coconut aminos
2 tablespoons rice vinegar
1 tablespoon grated peeled fresh ginger
1 tablespoon coconut sugar
¼ teaspoon red pepper flakes (optional)

1. Place a large skillet over medium-high heat. Season the steak strips with the salt and pepper. Add it to the skillet with the avocado oil, and stir-fry for 3 to 4 minutes until just cooked. Transfer to a plate. 2. Wipe out the skillet. Reduce the heat to medium and add the sesame oil and garlic. Cook, stirring occasionally, for 2 to 3 minutes. 3. Stir in the bok choy, coconut aminos, vinegar, ginger, coconut sugar, and red pepper flakes (if using) until well combined. Cover and cook for 2 minutes. 4. Add the steak to the skillet. Toss gently to combine and warm through, about 1 minute. Serve hot.

Per Serving

Calories: 252 | fat: 13g | protein: 19g | carbs: 12g | fiber: 9g | sugar: 3g | sodium: 349mg

Chapter 5 Poultry

58 **Chicken with Fennel and Zucchini**   44

59 **Russian Kotleti**   44

60 **Lemon and Garlic Chicken Thighs**   44

61 **Turkey Meatballs with Spaghetti Squash**   45

62 **Spicy Chicken Drumsticks**   45

63 **Comforting Chicken Stew**   46

64 **Sesame Chicken Stir-Fry**   46

65 **Rosemary Chicken**   46

66 **Chicken Lettuce Wraps**   48

67 **Chicken Skewers with Mint Sauce**   48

68 **Nutty Pesto Chicken Supreme**   49

69 **Herb-Roasted Chicken**   49

70 **Baked Chicken Breast with Lemon and Garlic**   49

71 **Turkey Sloppy Joes**   50

72 **Easy Turkey Breakfast Sausage**   50

Chicken with Fennel and Zucchini

Prep time: 15 minutes | Cook time: 15 minutes | Serves 4

2 tablespoons extra-virgin olive oil
4 boneless skinless chicken breasts, cut into strips
1 leek, white part only, sliced thinly
1 fennel bulb, sliced into ¼-inch rounds
3 zucchini, sliced into ½-inch rounds
½ cup chicken broth
1 teaspoon salt
½ teaspoon freshly ground black pepper
½ cup sliced green olives
2 tablespoons chopped fresh dill

1. In a large pan over high heat, heat the olive oil. 2. Add the chicken strips. Brown them for 1 to 2 minutes, stirring constantly. Transfer the chicken and its juices to a plate or bowl and set aside. 3. Add the leek, fennel, and zucchini to the pan. Sauté for 5 minutes. 4. Return the chicken and juices to the pan. Pour in the broth. Add the salt and pepper. Cover the pan and simmer for 5 minutes. 5. Remove the pan from the heat, and stir in the olives and dill.

Per Serving
Calories: 418 | fat: 20g | protein: 45g | carbs: 15g | fiber: 4g | sugar: 5g | sodium: 1021mg

Russian Kotleti

Prep time: 10 minutes | Cook time: 10 minutes | Serves 4

¼ cup filtered water
1 pound (454 g) ground chicken
½ small white onion, diced
1 egg, whisked
1 teaspoon salt
½ teaspoon garlic powder
½ teaspoon dried dill
½ teaspoon freshly ground black pepper
1 slice gluten-free bread
2 teaspoons ghee

1. In a medium bowl, combine the chicken, onion, egg, salt, garlic powder, dill, and pepper. Mix well with your hands. 2. In a small bowl, soak the bread in the water for 1 minute. 3. Add the soaked bread to the chicken mixture. With your hands, work to break it up as you mix it in. If you prefer, mix the ingredients in a stand mixer. 4. Divide the chicken mixture into 8 portions and roll each into a ball. Press them slightly to form short, thick patties. 5. In a large skillet over medium heat, heat the ghee. Place the patties in the pan so they do not touch, and cook for 5 minutes per side. Cut into one to check for doneness (no longer pink) before removing from the heat.

Per Serving
Calories: 213 | fat: 9g | protein: 24g | carbs: 9g | fiber: 1g | sugar: 0g | sodium: 618mg

Lemon and Garlic Chicken Thighs

Prep time: 15 minutes | Cook time: 7 to 8 hours | Serves 4 to 6

2 cups chicken broth
1½ teaspoons garlic powder
1 teaspoon sea salt
Juice and zest of 1 large lemon
2 pounds (907 g) boneless skinless chicken thighs

1. Pour the broth into the slow cooker. 2. In a small bowl, stir together the garlic powder, salt, lemon juice, and lemon zest. Baste each chicken thigh with an even coating of the mixture. Place the thighs along the bottom of the slow cooker. 3. Cover the cooker and set to low. Cook for 7 to 8 hours, or until the internal temperature of the chicken reaches 165ºF (74ºC) on a meat thermometer and the juices run clear, and serve.

Per Serving
Calories: 290 | fat: 14g | protein: 43g | carbs: 3g | fiber: 0g | sugar: 0g | sodium: 1017mg

Turkey Meatballs with Spaghetti Squash

Prep time: 15 minutes | Cook time: 6 to 7 hours | Serves 4 to 6

1 spaghetti squash, halved lengthwise and seeded

Sauce:

1 (15-ounce / 425-g) can diced tomatoes

½ teaspoon garlic powder

½ teaspoon dried oregano

½ teaspoon sea salt

Meatballs:

1 pound (454 g) ground turkey

1 large egg, whisked

½ small white onion, minced

1 teaspoon garlic powder

½ teaspoon sea salt

½ teaspoon dried oregano

½ teaspoon dried basil leaves

Freshly ground black pepper, to taste

To Begin:

1. Place the squash halves in the bottom of your slow cooker, cut-side down.

Make the Sauce:

1. Pour the diced tomatoes around the squash in the bottom of the slow cooker. 2. Sprinkle in the garlic powder, oregano, and salt.

Make the Meatballs:

1. In a medium bowl, mix together the turkey, egg, onion, garlic powder, salt, oregano, and basil, and season with pepper. Form the turkey mixture into 12 balls, and place them in the slow cooker around the spaghetti squash. 2. Cover the cooker and set to low. Cook for 6 to 7 hours. 3. Transfer the squash to a work surface, and use a fork to shred it into spaghetti-like strands. Combine the strands with the tomato sauce, top with the meatballs, and serve.

Per Serving

Calories: 253 | fat: 8g | protein: 24g | carbs: 22g | fiber: 1g | sugar: 4g | sodium: 948mg

Spicy Chicken Drumsticks

Prep time: 10 minutes | Cook time: 35 to 45 minutes | Serves 4 to 6

6 chicken drumsticks

1 cup unsweetened coconut yogurt

½ cup extra-virgin olive oil

Juice of 2 limes

2 garlic cloves, smashed

1 tablespoon raw honey

1 teaspoon salt

1 teaspoon ground cumin

½ teaspoon paprika

½ teaspoon ground turmeric

¼ teaspoon freshly ground black pepper

Olive oil cooking spray

1. Place the chicken in a shallow baking dish. 2. In a small bowl, whisk together the yogurt, olive oil, lime juice, garlic, honey, salt, cumin, paprika, turmeric, and pepper until smooth. 3. Pour the yogurt mixture over the chicken. Cover with plastic wrap and chill for 30 minutes, or overnight. 4. Preheat the oven to 375ºF (190ºC). 5. Line a rimmed baking sheet with aluminum foil and lightly grease it with cooking spray. 6. Remove the drumsticks from the marinade and place them on the prepared sheet. Discard the marinade. 7. Place the sheet in the preheated oven and bake the drumsticks for 25 to 35 minutes, or until they start to brown and are cooked through.

Per Serving

Calories: 380 | fat: 31g | protein: 19g | carbs: 9g | fiber: 2g | sugar: 5g | sodium: 686mg

Comforting Chicken Stew

Prep time: 15 minutes | Cook time: 4 hours | Serves 4 to 6

1 tablespoon extra-virgin olive oil
3 pounds (1.4 kg) boneless, skinless chicken thighs
1 large onion, thinly sliced
2 garlic cloves, thinly sliced
1 teaspoon minced fresh ginger root
2 teaspoons ground turmeric
1 teaspoon whole coriander seeds, lightly crushed
1 teaspoon salt
¼ teaspoon freshly ground black pepper
2 cups chicken broth
1 cup unsweetened coconut milk
¼ cup chopped fresh cilantro (optional)

1. Drizzle the oil into a slow cooker. 2. Add the chicken, onion, garlic, ginger root, turmeric, coriander, salt, pepper, chicken broth, and coconut milk, and toss to combine. 3. Cover and cook on high for 4 hours. Garnish with the chopped cilantro (if using) and serve.

Per Serving
Calories: 370 | fat: 19g | protein: 46g | carbs: 4g | fiber: 1g | sugar: 1g | sodium: 770mg

Sesame Chicken Stir-Fry

Prep time: 15 minutes | Cook time: 25 minutes | Serves 6

¾ cup warm water
½ cup tahini
¼ cup plus 2 tablespoons toasted sesame oil, divided
2 garlic cloves, minced
½ teaspoon salt
1 pound (454 g) boneless skinless chicken breasts, cut into ½-inch cubes
6 cups lightly packed kale, thoroughly washed and chopped

1. In a medium bowl, whisk together the warm water, tahini, ¼ cup of sesame oil, garlic, and salt. 2. In a large pan set over medium heat, heat the remaining 2 tablespoons of sesame oil. 3. Add the chicken and cook for 8 to 10 minutes, stirring. 4. Stir in the tahini-sesame sauce, mixing well to coat the chicken. Cook for 6 to 8 minutes more. 5. One handful at a time, add the kale. When the first handful wilts, add the next. Continue until all the kale has been added. Serve hot.

Per Serving
Calories: 417 | fat: 30g | protein: 27g | carbs: 12g | fiber: 3g | sugar: 0g | sodium: 311mg

Rosemary Chicken

Prep time: 10 minutes | Cook time: 20 minutes | Serves 4

1½ pounds (680 g) chicken breast tenders
2 tablespoons extra-virgin olive oil
2 tablespoons chopped fresh rosemary leaves
½ teaspoon sea salt
⅛ teaspoon freshly ground black pepper

1. Preheat the oven to 425ºF (220ºC). 2. Place the chicken tenders on a rimmed baking sheet. Brush them with the olive oil and sprinkle with the rosemary, salt, and pepper. 3. Bake for 15 to 20 minutes, or until the juices run clear.

Per Serving
Calories: 389 | fat: 20g | protein: 49g | carbs: 1g | fiber: 0g | sugar: 0g | sodium: 381mg

Chicken Lettuce Wraps

Prep time: 20 minutes | Cook time: 0 minutes | Serves 4

2 heads butter lettuce, 8 lettuce cups total
1 pound (454 g) grilled boneless skin-on chicken breast, cut into ½-inch cubes
1 cup shredded carrots
½ cup thinly sliced radishes
2 scallions, sliced thinly
2 tablespoons chopped fresh cilantro
½ cup toasted sesame oil
3 tablespoons freshly squeezed lime juice
1 tablespoon coconut aminos
1 garlic clove
1 thin slice fresh ginger
1 teaspoon lime zest
1 tablespoon sesame seeds, divided

1. Place the lettuce cups on a serving platter. 2. Evenly divide the chicken, carrots, radishes, scallions, and cilantro among the lettuce cups. 3. In a blender or food processor, combine the sesame oil, lime juice, coconut aminos, garlic, ginger, and lime zest. Blend until smooth. 4. Drizzle the chicken and vegetables with the dressing and sprinkle each with sesame seeds.

Per Serving

Calories: 342 | fat: 30g | protein: 7g | carbs: 13g | fiber: 3g | sugar: 4g | sodium: 40mg

Chicken Skewers with Mint Sauce

Prep time: 20 minutes | Cook time: 20 minutes | Serves 4 to 6

Mint Sauce:
1 bunch fresh mint, stemmed
½ cup extra-virgin olive oil
1 garlic clove
2 teaspoons lemon zest
½ teaspoon salt
Pinch freshly ground black pepper

Chicken:
6 boneless skinless chicken breasts, cut into 1½- to 2-inch cubes
¼ cup extra-virgin olive oil
¼ cup freshly squeezed lemon juice
1 teaspoon salt
¼ teaspoon freshly ground black pepper
Pinch ground turmeric
2 fresh mint sprigs

Make the Mint Sauce:

1. In a blender or food processor, combine the mint, olive oil, garlic, lemon zest, salt, and pepper. Blend until smooth. 2. Refrigerate in an airtight container for no more than four or five days.

Make the Chicken:

1. Soak 12 (6-inch) wooden skewers in water for at least 30 minutes so the skewers won't burn while on the grill. 2. In a large zip-top plastic bag, combine the chicken, olive oil, lemon juice, salt, pepper, turmeric, and mint. Close the bag, refrigerate, turn to coat, and let marinate at least 30 minutes, or overnight. 3. Preheat the grill, or place a stovetop grill over high heat. 4. Put 3 or 4 chicken cubes on each skewer. Discard the marinade and mint sprigs. 5. Reduce the grill to medium. Grill the chicken for 15 to 20 minutes, turning occasionally, until each skewer is marked on both sides and the chicken is cooked through. 6. Serve with the mint sauce.

Per Serving

Calories: 657 | fat: 51g | protein: 50g | carbs: 2g | fiber: 1g | sugar: 0g | sodium: 1024mg

Nutty Pesto Chicken Supreme

Prep time: 10 minutes | Cook time: 30 minutes | Serves 4

2 free range skinless chicken or turkey breasts
1 bunch of fresh basil
½ cup raw spinach
1 cup crushed macadamias, Almonds, walnuts or a combination
2 tablespoons extra virgin olive oil

1. Preheat oven to 350ºF (180ºC). 2. Take the chicken breasts and use a meat pounder to 'thin' each breast into a 1cm thick escalope. 3. Reserve a handful of the nuts before adding the rest of the ingredients and a little black pepper to a blender or pestle and mortar and blend until smooth (you can leave this a little chunky for a rustic feel if you wish). 4. Add a little water if the pesto needs loosening. 5. Coat the chicken in the pesto. 6. Bake for at least 30 minutes in the oven, or until chicken is completely cooked through. 7. Top each chicken escalope with the remaining nuts and place under the broiler for 5 minutes for a crispy topping to complete.

Per Serving
Calories: 445 | fat: 35g | protein: 30g | carbs: 5g | fiber: 3g | sugar: 2g | sodium: 65mg

Herb-Roasted Chicken

Prep time: 15 minutes | Cook time: 1 hour 30 minutes | Serves 4

1 (4-pound / 1.8-kg) whole chicken, rinsed and patted dry
2 lemons, halved
1 sweet onion, quartered
4 garlic cloves, crushed
6 fresh thyme sprigs
6 fresh rosemary sprigs
3 bay leaves
2 tablespoons olive oil
Sea salt, to taste
Freshly ground black pepper, to taste

1. Preheat the oven to 400ºF (205ºC). 2. Place the chicken in a roasting pan. Stuff the lemons, onion, garlic, thyme, rosemary, and bay leaves into the cavity. Brush the chicken with the olive oil, and season lightly with sea salt and pepper. 3. Roast the chicken for about 1½ hours until golden brown and cooked through. 4. Remove the chicken from the oven and let it sit for 10 minutes. Remove the lemons, onion, and herbs from the cavity and serve.

Per Serving
Calories: 261 | fat: 9g | protein: 38g | carbs: 5g | fiber: 2g | sugar: 2g | sodium: 325mg

Baked Chicken Breast with Lemon and Garlic

Prep time: 5 minutes | Cook time: 20 to 25 minutes | Serves 4

Juice of 1 lemon
Zest of 1 lemon
1 teaspoon garlic powder
½ teaspoon salt
3 tablespoons avocado oil
2 (8-ounce / 227-g) boneless, skinless chicken breasts

1. Preheat the oven to 375ºF (190ºC). 2. In a small bowl, mix the lemon juice, lemon zest, garlic powder, and salt. Set aside. 3. With a basting brush, spread 1½ tablespoons of avocado oil on the bottom of a glass or ceramic baking dish and brush them thoroughly with the chicken breasts in the dish. Brush the remaining 1½ tablespoons of avocado oil. 4. With the brush, coat the chicken with the lemon-garlic mixture. 5. Bake for 20 to 25 minutes, or until the center of the chicken reaches 165ºF (74ºC) on an instant-read thermometer.

Per Serving
Calories: 208 | fat: 12g | protein: 23g | carbs: 2g | fiber: 0g | sugar: 0g | sodium: 383mg

Turkey Sloppy Joes

Prep time: 15 minutes | Cook time: 4 to 6 hours | Serves 4 to 6

1 tablespoon extra-virgin olive oil
1 pound (454 g) ground turkey
1 celery stalk, minced
1 carrot, minced
½ medium sweet onion, diced
½ red bell pepper, finely chopped
6 tablespoons tomato paste
2 tablespoons apple cider vinegar
1 tablespoon maple syrup
1 teaspoon Dijon mustard
1 teaspoon chili powder
½ teaspoon garlic powder
½ teaspoon sea salt
½ teaspoon dried oregano

1. In your slow cooker, combine the olive oil, turkey, celery, carrot, onion, red bell pepper, tomato paste, vinegar, maple syrup, mustard, chili powder, garlic powder, salt, and oregano. Using a large spoon, break up the turkey into smaller chunks as it combines with the other ingredients. 2. Cover the cooker and set to low. Cook for 4 to 6 hours, stir thoroughly, and serve.

Per Serving
Calories: 251 | fat: 12g | protein: 24g | carbs: 14g | fiber: 3g | sugar: 9g | sodium: 690mg

Easy Turkey Breakfast Sausage

Prep time: 15 minutes | Cook time: 15 minutes | Serves 4

Extra-virgin olive oil, for brushing
1½ pounds (680 g) ground turkey
1 teaspoon salt
½ teaspoon freshly ground black pepper
½ teaspoon ground nutmeg
1 tablespoon chopped fresh sage
2 scallions, sliced
½ cup dried blueberries

1. Preheat the oven to 400ºF (205ºC). 2. Brush a rimmed baking sheet with olive oil. 3. In a medium bowl, mix together the turkey, salt, pepper, nutmeg, sage, scallions, and blueberries; it may be easiest to do this with your hands. 4. Using a small (1-ounce / 28-g) ice cream scoop, scoop the mixture onto the prepared baking sheet. With your fingers or the back of a spatula, gently flatten the mounds into a patty shape. 5. Place the sheet in the preheated oven and bake for 10 to 15 minutes, or until firm to the touch.

Per Serving
Calories: 348 | fat: 19g | protein: 47g | carbs: 4g | fiber: 1g | sugar: 2g | sodium: 765mg

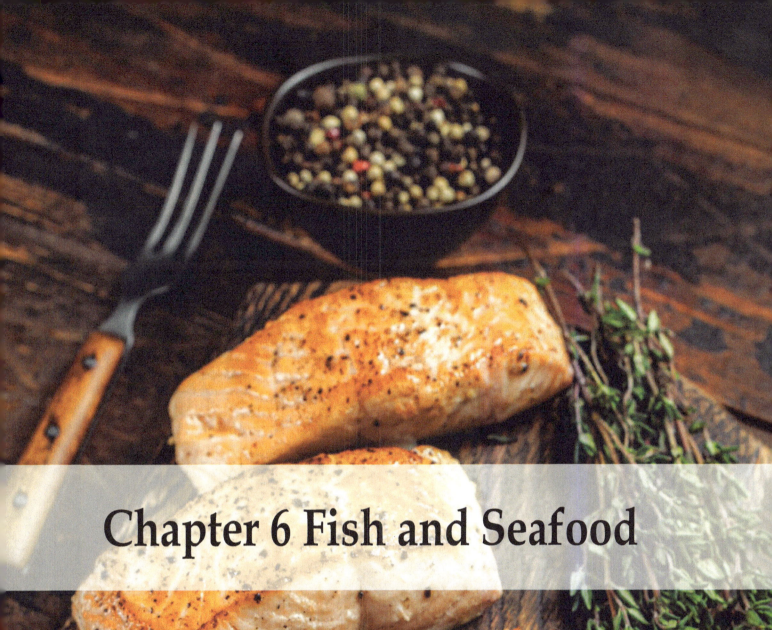

Chapter 6 Fish and Seafood

- **73** Seared Scallops with Greens 53
- **74** Whitefish Chowder 53
- **75** Quinoa Salmon Bowl 53
- **76** Manhattan-Style Salmon Chowder 54
- **77** Miso-Glazed Salmon 54
- **78** Coconut-Crusted Shrimp 54
- **79** Baked Salmon with Oregano Pistou 55
- **80** Coconut Milk-Baked Sole 55
- **81** Orange and Maple-Glazed Salmon 57
- **82** Ginger and Chili Sea Bass Fillets 57
- **83** Lime-Salmon Patties 57
- **84** Sautéed Sardines with Cauliflower Mash 58
- **85** Grilled Salmon Packets with Asparagus 58
- **86** Rosemary-Lemon Cod 58
- **87** Baked Salmon Patties with Greens 59
- **88** Fresh Tuna Steak and Fennel Salad 59
- **89** Sardine Donburi 59

Seared Scallops with Greens

Prep time: 20 minutes | Cook time: 15 minutes | Serves 4

1½ pounds (680 g) sea scallops, cleaned and patted dry
Sea salt, to taste
Freshly ground black pepper, to taste
2 tablespoons olive oil, divided

2 garlic cloves, thinly sliced
2 cups chopped kale leaves
2 cups fresh spinach

1. Lightly season the scallops all over with sea salt and pepper. 2. Place a large skillet over medium-high heat and add 1 tablespoon of olive oil. 3. Pan-sear the scallops for about 2 minutes per side, or until opaque and just cooked through. Transfer to a plate and cover loosely with aluminum foil to keep them warm. Wipe the skillet with a paper towel and place it back on the heat. 4. Add the remaining 1 tablespoon of olive oil to the skillet and sauté the garlic for about 4 minutes, or until caramelized. 5. Stir in the kale and spinach. Cook, tossing with tongs, for about 6 minutes, or until the greens are tender and wilted. 6. Divide the greens with any juices equally among four plates and top each with the scallops.

Per Serving
Calories: 232 | fat: 8g | protein: 30g | carbs: 9g | fiber: 1g | sugar: 0g | sodium: 682mg

Whitefish Chowder

Prep time: 10 minutes | Cook time: 35 minutes | Serves 8

4 carrots, peeled and cut into ½-inch pieces
3 sweet potatoes, peeled and cut into ½-inch pieces
3 cups full-fat coconut milk
2 cups water

1 teaspoon dried thyme
½ teaspoon salt
10½ ounces (298 g) white fish, skinless and firm, such as cod or halibut, cut into chunks

1. In a large pot, combine the carrots, sweet potatoes, coconut milk, water, thyme, and salt. Bring to a boil over high heat. Reduce the heat to low. Cover and simmer for 20 minutes. 2. In a blender, purée half of the soup. Return the purée to the pot. Add the fish chunks. 3. Cook for 12 to 15 minutes more, or until the fish is tender and hot.

Per Serving
Calories: 451 | fat: 29g | protein: 14g | carbs: 39g | fiber: 8g | sugar: 7g | sodium: 251mg

Quinoa Salmon Bowl

Prep time: 15 minutes | Cook time: 0 minutes | Serves 4

4 cups cooked quinoa
1 pound (454 g) cooked salmon, flaked
3 cups arugula
6 radishes, thinly sliced
1 zucchini, sliced into half moons
3 scallions, minced

½ cup almond oil
1 tablespoon apple cider vinegar
1 teaspoon Sriracha or other hot sauce (or more if you like it spicy)
1 teaspoon salt
½ cup toasted slivered almonds (optional)

1. Combine the quinoa, salmon, arugula, radishes, zucchini, and scallions in a large bowl. 2. Add the almond oil, vinegar, Sriracha, and salt and mix well. 3. Divide the mixture among four serving bowls, garnish with the toasted almonds (if using), and serve.

Per Serving
Calories: 790 | fat: 52g | protein: 37g | carbs: 45g | fiber: 8g | sugar: 4g | sodium: 680mg

Manhattan-Style Salmon Chowder

Prep time: 10 minutes | Cook time: 15 minutes | Serves 4

¼ cup extra-virgin olive oil
1 red bell pepper, chopped
1 pound (454 g) skinless salmon, pin bones removed, and chopped into ½-inch pieces
2 (28 ounces / 794 g) cans crushed tomatoes, 1 drained and 1 undrained

6 cups no-salt-added chicken broth
2 cups diced sweet potatoes
1 teaspoon onion powder
½ teaspoon sea salt
¼ teaspoon freshly ground black pepper

1. In a large pot over medium-high heat, heat the olive oil until it shimmers. 2. Add the red bell pepper and salmon. Cook for about 5 minutes, stirring occasionally, until the fish is opaque and the bell pepper is soft. 3. Stir in the tomatoes, chicken broth, sweet potatoes, onion powder, salt, and pepper. Bring to a simmer and reduce the heat to medium. Cook for about 10 minutes, stirring occasionally, until the sweet potatoes are soft.

Per Serving
Calories: 570 | fat: 39g | protein: 41g | carbs: 55g | fiber: 16g | sugar: 24g | sodium: 600mg

Miso-Glazed Salmon

Prep time: 5 minutes | Cook time: 5 to 10 minutes | Serves 4

4 (4-ounce / 113-g) salmon fillets
3 tablespoons miso paste
2 tablespoons raw honey

1 teaspoon coconut aminos
1 teaspoon rice vinegar

1. Preheat the broiler. 2. Line a baking dish with aluminum foil and place the salmon fillets in it. 3. In a small bowl, stir together the miso, honey, coconut aminos, and vinegar. Brush the glaze evenly over the top of each fillet. Broil for about 5 minutes. The fish is done when it flakes easily. The exact cooking time depends on its thickness. 4. Brush any remaining glaze over the fish, and continue to broil for 5 minutes, if needed.

Per Serving
Calories: 264 | fat: 9g | protein: 30g | carbs: 13g | fiber: 0g | sugar: 9g | sodium: 716mg

Coconut-Crusted Shrimp

Prep time: 10 minutes | Cook time: 6 minutes | Serves 4

2 eggs
1 cup unsweetened dried coconut
¼ cup coconut flour
½ teaspoon salt
¼ teaspoon paprika

Dash cayenne pepper
Dash freshly ground black pepper
¼ cup coconut oil
1 pound (454 g) raw shrimp, peeled and deveined

1. In a small shallow bowl, whisk the eggs. 2. In another small shallow bowl, mix the coconut, coconut flour, salt, paprika, cayenne pepper, and black pepper. 3. In a large skillet over medium-high heat, heat the coconut oil. 4. Pat the shrimp dry with a paper towel. 5. Working one at a time, hold each shrimp by the tail, dip it into the egg mixture, and then into the coconut mixture until coated. Place into the hot skillet. Cook for 1 to 3 minutes per side. Transfer to a paper towel-lined plate to drain excess oil. 6. Serve immediately.

Per Serving
Calories: 279 | fat: 20g | protein: 19g | carbs: 6g | fiber: 3g | sugar: 2g | sodium: 481mg

Baked Salmon with Oregano Pistou

Prep time: 10 minutes | Cook time: 20 minutes | Serves 4

Pistou:

1 cup fresh oregano leaves
¼ cup almonds
2 garlic cloves
Juice of 1 lime (1 or 2 tablespoons)

Zest of 1 lime (optional)
1 tablespoon olive oil
Pinch sea salt

Fish:

4 (6-ounce / 170-g) salmon fillets
Sea salt, to taste

Freshly ground black pepper, to taste
1 tablespoon olive oil

Make the Pistou:

1. In a blender, combine the oregano, almonds, garlic, lime juice, lime zest (if using), olive oil, and sea salt. Pulse until very finely chopped. Transfer the pistou to a bowl and set it aside.

Make the Fish:

1. Preheat the oven to 400°F (205°C). 2. Lightly season the salmon with sea salt and pepper. 3. Place a large ovenproof skillet over medium-high heat and add the olive oil. 4. Add the salmon and pan-sear for 4 minutes per side. 5. Place the skillet in the oven and bake the fish for about 10 minutes, or until it is just cooked through. 6. Serve the salmon topped with a spoonful of pistou.

Per Serving

Calories: 377 | fat: 22g | protein: 36g | carbs: 13g | fiber: 9g | sugar: 0g | sodium: 239mg

Coconut Milk-Baked Sole

Prep time: 20 minutes | Cook time: 20 minutes | Serves 4

2 tablespoons warm water
Pinch saffron threads
2 pounds (907 g) sole fillets
Sea salt, to taste
2 tablespoons freshly squeezed lemon juice
1 tablespoon coconut oil

1 sweet onion, chopped, or about 1 cup precut packaged onion
2 teaspoons bottled minced garlic
1 teaspoon grated fresh ginger
1 cup canned full-fat coconut milk
2 tablespoons chopped fresh cilantro

1. Place the water in a small bowl and sprinkle the saffron threads on top. Let it stand for 10 minutes. 2. Preheat the oven to 350°F (180°C). 3. Rub the fish with sea salt and the lemon juice, and place the fillets in a 9-by-9-inch baking dish. Roast the fish for 10 minutes. 4. While the fish is roasting, place a large skillet over medium-high heat and add the coconut oil. 5. Add the onion, garlic, and ginger. Sauté for about 3 minutes, or until softened. 6. Stir in the coconut milk and the saffron water. Bring to a boil. Reduce the heat to low and simmer the sauce for 5 minutes. Remove the skillet from the heat. 7. Pour the sauce over the fish. Cover and bake for about 10 minutes, or until the fish flakes easily with a fork. 8. Serve the fish topped with the cilantro.

Per Serving

Calories: 449 | fat: 21g | protein: 56g | carbs: 7g | fiber: 2g | sugar: 4g | sodium: 1028mg

Orange and Maple-Glazed Salmon

Prep time: 15 minutes | Cook time: 15 minutes | Serves 4

Juice of 2 oranges
Zest of 1 orange
¼ cup pure maple syrup
2 tablespoons low-sodium soy sauce
1 teaspoon garlic powder
4 (4- to 6-ounce / 113- to 170-g) salmon fillets, pin bones removed

1. Preheat the oven to 400ºF (205ºC). 2. In a small, shallow dish, whisk the orange juice and zest, maple syrup, soy sauce, and garlic powder. 3. Put the salmon pieces, flesh-side down, into the dish. Let it marinate for 10 minutes. 4. Transfer the salmon, skin-side up, to a rimmed baking sheet and bake for about 15 minutes until the flesh is opaque.

Per Serving
Calories: 297 | fat: 11g | protein: 34g | carbs: 18g | fiber: 1g | sugar: 15g | sodium: 528mg

Ginger and Chili Sea Bass Fillets

Prep time: 10 minutes | Cook time: 10 minutes | Serves 2

2 sea bass fillets
1 teaspoon black pepper
1 tablespoon extra virgin olive oil
1 teaspoon ginger, peeled and chopped
1 garlic clove, thinly sliced
1 red chili, deseeded and thinly sliced
2 green onion stems, sliced

1. Get a skillet and heat the oil on a medium to high heat. 2. Sprinkle black pepper over the sea bass and score the skin of the fish a few times with a sharp knife. 3. Add the sea bass fillet to the very hot pan with the skin side down. 4. Cook for 5 minutes and turn over. 5. Cook for a further 2 minutes. 6. Remove sea bass from the pan and rest. 7. Add the chili, garlic and ginger and cook for approximately 2 minutes or until golden. 8. Remove from the heat and add the green onions. 9. Scatter the vegetables over your sea bass to serve.

Per Serving
Calories: 204 | fat: 10g | protein: 25g | carbs: 4g | fiber: 1g | sugar: 2g | sodium: 92mg

Lime-Salmon Patties

Prep time: 20 minutes | Cook time: 10 minutes | Serves 4

½ pound (227 g) cooked boneless salmon fillet, flaked
2 eggs
¾ cup almond flour, plus more as needed
1 scallion, white and green parts, chopped
Juice of 2 limes (2 to 4 tablespoons), plus more as needed
Zest of 2 limes (optional)
1 tablespoon chopped fresh dill
Pinch sea salt
1 tablespoon olive oil
1 lime, cut into wedges

1. In a large bowl, mix together the salmon, eggs, almond flour, scallion, lime juice, lime zest (if using), dill, and sea salt until the mixture holds together when pressed. If the mixture is too dry, add more lime juice; if it is too wet, add more almond flour. 2. Divide the salmon mixture into 4 equal portions, and press them into patties about ½ inch thick. Refrigerate them for about 30 minutes to firm up. 3. Place a large skillet over medium-high heat and add the olive oil. 4. Add the salmon patties and brown for about 5 minutes per side, turning once. 5. Serve the patties with lime wedges.

Per Serving
Calories: 243 | fat: 18g | protein: 18g | carbs: 5g | fiber: 2g | sugar: 0g | sodium: 84mg

Sautéed Sardines with Cauliflower Mash

Prep time: 10 minutes | Cook time: 15 minutes | Serves 4

2 heads cauliflower, broken into large florets
4 tablespoons extra-virgin olive oil, divided
¼ teaspoon salt
4 (4-ounce / 113-g) cans sardines packed in water, drained
1 cup fresh parsley, finely chopped

1. Fill a large pot with 2 inches of water and insert a steamer basket. Bring the water to a boil over high heat. 2. Add the cauliflower to the basket. Cover and steam for 8 to 10 minutes, or until the florets are tender. Transfer the cauliflower to a food processor. 3. Add 2 tablespoons of olive oil and the salt to the cauliflower. Process until the cauliflower is smooth and creamy. Depending on the size of your processor, you may need to do this in two batches. 4. In a medium bowl, roughly mash the sardines. 5. Add the remaining 2 tablespoons of olive oil to a medium pan set over low heat. When oil is shimmering, add the sardines and parsley. Cook for 3 minutes. You want the sardines to be warm, not scalding hot. 6. Serve the sardines with a generous scoop of cauliflower mash.

Per Serving

Calories: 334 | fat: 24g | protein: 26g | carbs: 8g | fiber: 4g | sugar: 3g | sodium: 465mg

Grilled Salmon Packets with Asparagus

Prep time: 15 minutes | Cook time: 20 minutes | Serves 4

4 (4-ounce / 113-g) skinless salmon fillets
16 asparagus spears, tough ends trimmed
4 tablespoons avocado oil, divided
1 teaspoon garlic powder, divided
½ teaspoon salt, divided
Freshly ground black pepper, to taste
1 lemon, thinly sliced

1. Preheat the oven to 400ºF (205ºC). 2. Cut 4 (12-inch) squares of parchment paper or foil and put on a work surface. 3. Place 1 salmon fillet in the center of each square and 4 asparagus spears next to each fillet. Brush the fish and asparagus with 1 tablespoon of avocado oil. 4. Sprinkle each fillet with ¼ teaspoon garlic powder and ⅛ teaspoon salt, and season with pepper. 5. Place the lemon slices on top of the fillets. Close and seal the parchment around each fillet so it forms a sealed packet. 6. Place the parchment packets on a baking sheet. Bake for 20 minutes. 7. Place a sealed parchment packet on each of 4 plates and serve hot.

Per Serving

Calories: 339 | fat: 23g | protein: 30g | carbs: 1g | fiber: 1g | sugar: 0g | sodium: 530mg

Rosemary-Lemon Cod

Prep time: 10 minutes | Cook time: 11 minutes | Serves 4

2 tablespoons extra-virgin olive oil
1½ pounds (680 g) cod, skin and bones removed, cut into 4 fillets
1 tablespoon chopped fresh rosemary leaves
½ teaspoon freshly ground black pepper, or more to taste
½ teaspoon sea salt
Juice of 1 lemon

1. In a large nonstick skillet over medium-high heat, heat the olive oil until it shimmers. 2. Season the cod with the rosemary, pepper, and salt. Add the fish to the skillet and cook for 3 to 5 minutes per side until opaque. 3. Pour the lemon juice over the cod fillets and cook for 1 minute.

Per Serving

Calories: 246 | fat: 9g | protein: 39g | carbs: 1g | fiber: 0g | sugar: 0g | sodium: 370mg

Baked Salmon Patties with Greens

Prep time: 15 minutes | Cook time: 38 minutes | Serves 4

2 cups cooked, mashed sweet potatoes (about 2 large sweet potatoes)
2 (6-ounce / 170-g) cans wild salmon, drained
¼ cup almond flour
¼ teaspoon ground turmeric
2 tablespoons coconut oil
2 kale bunches, thoroughly washed, stemmed, and cut into ribbons
¼ teaspoon salt

1. Preheat the oven to 350ºF (180ºC). 2. Line a baking sheet with parchment paper. 3. In a large bowl, stir together the mashed sweet potatoes and salmon. 4. Blend in the almond flour and turmeric. 5. Using a ⅓-cup measure, scoop the salmon mixture onto the baking sheet. Flatten slightly with the bottom of the measuring cup. Repeat with the remaining mixture. 6. Place the sheet in the preheated oven and bake for 30 minutes, flip-ping the patties halfway through. 7. In a large pan set over medium heat, heat the coconut oil. 8. Add the kale. Sauté for 5 to 8 minutes, or until the kale is bright and wilted. Sprinkle with the salt and serve with the salmon patties.

Per Serving
Calories: 320 | fat: 13g | protein: 21g | carbs: 32g | fiber: 5g | sugar: 0g | sodium: 88mg

Fresh Tuna Steak and Fennel Salad

Prep time: 15 minutes | Cook time: 25 minutes | Serves 4

2 (1 inch) tuna steaks
2 tablespoons olive oil, 1 tablespoon olive oil for brushing
1 teaspoon crushed black peppercorns
1 teaspoon crushed fennel seeds
1 fennel bulb, trimmed and sliced
½ cup water
1 lemon, juiced
1 teaspoon fresh parsley, chopped

1. Coat the fish with oil and then season with peppercorns and fennel seeds. 2. Heat the oil on a medium heat and sauté the fennel bulb slices for 5 minutes or until light brown. 3. Add the water to the pan and cook for 10 minutes until fennel is tender. 4. Stir in the lemon juice and lower heat to a simmer. 5. Meanwhile, heat another skillet and sauté the tuna steaks for about 2 to 3 minutes each side for medium-rare. (Add 1 minute each side for medium and 2 minutes each side for medium well). 6. Serve the fennel mix with the tuna steaks on top and garnish with the fresh parsley.

Per Serving
Calories: 288 | fat: 9g | protein: 44g | carbs: 6g | fiber: 2g | sugar: 3g | sodium: 105mg

Sardine Donburi

Prep time: 10 minutes | Cook time: 50 minutes | Serves 6

2 cups brown rice, rinsed well
4 cups water
½ teaspoon salt
3 (4-ounce / 113-g) cans sardines packed in water,
drained
3 scallions, sliced thin
1 (1-inch) piece fresh ginger, grated
4 tablespoons sesame oil, or extra-virgin olive oil, divided

1. In a large pot, combine the rice, water, and salt. Bring to a boil over high heat. Reduce the heat to low. Cover and cook for 45 to 50 minutes, or until tender. 2. In a medium bowl, roughly mash the sardines. 3. When the rice is done, add the sardines, scallions, and ginger to the pot. Mix thoroughly. 4. Divide the rice among four bowls. Drizzle each bowl with 1 teaspoon to 1 tablespoon of sesame oil.

Per Serving
Calories: 604 | fat: 24g | protein: 25g | carbs: 74g | fiber: 4g | sugar: 0g | sodium: 499mg

Chapter 7 Salads

90 **Sautéed Ginger and Bok Choy** 62

91 **Mackerel and Beetroot Super Salad** 62

92 **Simple Spinach Salad** 62

93 **Watermelon-Cucumber Salad** 64

94 **Chopped Thai Salad** 64

95 **Stone Fruit Salad** 65

96 **Creamy Cabbage Slaw** 65

97 **Mediterranean Chopped Salad** 65

98 **Massaged Swiss Chard Salad with Chopped Egg** 66

99 **Coconut Fruit Salad** 66

100 **On-The-Go Taco Salad** 67

101 **Shredded Root Vegetable Salad** 67

102 **Grapefruit-Avocado Salad** 68

103 **Cumin and mango chicken salad** 68

104 **Pear-Walnut Salad** 68

105 **Wild Rice Salad with Mushrooms** 69

106 **Massaged Kale Salad** 69

107 **Carrot and Raisin Salad** 69

Sautéed Ginger and Bok Choy

Prep time: 10 minutes | Cook time: 10 to 15 minutes | Serves 4

1 tablespoon sesame oil
2 garlic cloves, minced
1 teaspoon minced peeled fresh ginger
3 tablespoons filtered water
2 tablespoons coconut aminos
1 teaspoon rice vinegar
¼ teaspoon red pepper flakes
4 heads bok choy, halved lengthwise

1. In a large saucepan over medium heat, warm the sesame oil. 2. Add the garlic and ginger, and sauté for 2 minutes. 3. Stir in the water, coconut aminos, vinegar, and red pepper flakes. 4. Add the bok choy, cut-sides down, to the pan and cover. Lower the heat to low and let steam for 5 to 10 minutes. Once tender, remove from the heat and serve.

Per Serving
Calories: 143 | fat: 5g | protein: 12g | carbs: 21g | fiber: 8g | sugar: 10g | sodium: 65mg

Mackerel and Beetroot Super Salad

Prep time: 15 minutes | Cook time: 20 minutes | Serves 4

1 cup sweet potatoes, peeled
12 ounces (340 g) smoked mackerel fillets, skin removed
2 green onions, finely sliced
1 cup cooked beetroot, sliced into wedges
2 tablespoons bunch dill, finely chopped
2 tablespoons olive oil
Juice 1 lemon, zest of half
1 teaspoon caraway seeds, crushed using pestle and mortar
Pinch of black pepper

1. Place the potatoes in a small saucepan of boiling water and simmer for 15 minutes on a medium high heat or until fork-tender. 2. Cool and cut into thick slices. 3. Flake the mackerel into a bowl and add the cooled potatoes, green onions, beetroot and dill. 4. In a separate bowl, whisk together the olive oil, lemon juice, caraway seeds and black pepper. 5. Pour over the salad and toss well to coat. 6. Scatter over the lemon zest. 7. Pack into plastic containers and chill for later, or enjoy straight away.

Per Serving
Calories: 417 | fat: 18g | protein: 38g | carbs: 26g | fiber: 6g | sugar: 8g | sodium: 362mg

Simple Spinach Salad

Prep time: 10 minutes | Cook time: 0 minutes | Serves 4

¼ cup extra-virgin olive oil
¼ cup Dijon mustard
2 tablespoons freshly squeezed lemon juice
1½ tablespoons maple syrup
¼ teaspoon sea salt, plus additional as needed
6 cups baby spinach leaves

1. In a small jar, combine the olive oil, Dijon mustard, lemon juice, maple syrup, and salt. Cover and shake well to mix. 2. Taste, and adjust the seasoning if necessary. 3. In a large serving bowl, toss together the spinach and dressing. 4. Ingredient Tip: If you have extra vegetables or greens in the refrigerator, add them to this dish. Also, a sprinkle of walnuts or sunflower seeds, some dried fruit like dates or cranberries, or fresh fruit such as figs or raspberries add a nice touch.

Per Serving
Calories: 150 | fat: 14g | protein: 2g | carbs: 8g | fiber: 2g | sugar: 5g | sodium: 362mg

Watermelon-Cucumber Salad

Prep time: 25 minutes | Cook time: 0 minutes | Serves 4

Dressing:
½ cup olive oil
¼ cup apple cider vinegar
2 tablespoons raw honey
1 teaspoon freshly grated lemon zest (optional)
Pinch sea salt

Salad:
4 cups (½-inch) watermelon cubes
1 English cucumber, cut into ½-inch cubes
1 cup halved snow peas
1 scallion, white and green parts, chopped
2 cups shredded kale
1 tablespoon chopped fresh cilantro

Make the Dressing:
1. In a small bowl, whisk the olive oil, cider vinegar, honey, and lemon zest (if using). Season with sea salt and set it aside.

Make the Salad:
1. In a large bowl, toss together the watermelon, cucumber, snow peas, scallion, and dressing. 2. Divide the kale among four plates and top with the water-melon mixture. 3. Serve garnished with the cilantro.

Per Serving
Calories: 353 | fat: 26g | protein: 4g | carbs: 30g | fiber: 3g | sugar: 19g | sodium: 7mg

Chopped Thai Salad

Prep time: 25 minutes | Cook time: 0 minutes | Serves 6

Dressing:
½ cup extra-virgin olive oil
3 tablespoons filtered water
2 tablespoons coconut aminos
1 tablespoon apple cider vinegar
1 tablespoon freshly squeezed lime juice
1 tablespoon raw honey
1 teaspoon sesame oil
1 teaspoon garlic powder
Dash ground ginger

Salad:
2 cups shredded kale, stemmed and thoroughly washed
2 cups shredded napa cabbage
2 cups shredded red cabbage
4 scallions, sliced
1 cup shredded carrots
1 red bell pepper, julienned
1 yellow bell pepper, julienned
1 cucumber, julienned
½ cup fresh cilantro leaves, roughly chopped
½ cup cashews, roughly chopped

Make the Dressing: In a medium bowl, whisk the olive oil, water, coconut aminos, vinegar, lime juice, honey, sesame oil, garlic powder, and ginger until combined. Set aside.

Make the Salad:
1. In a large bowl, mix the kale, napa cabbage, red cabbage, scallions, carrots, red bell pepper, yellow bell pepper, and cucumber. 2. Top with the cilantro and cashews. 3. Pour the dressing over the salad, toss well, and serve immediately.

Per Serving
Calories: 272 | fat: 22g | protein: 3g | carbs: 16g | fiber: 4g | sugar: 7g | sodium: 40mg

Stone Fruit Salad

Prep time: 15 minutes | Cook time: 0 minutes | Serves 6

4 cups mixed chopped greens
1 cup sliced fresh peaches
1 cup fresh cherries, pitted and halved
1 cup sliced fresh nectarines
½ cup pecans, chopped
¼ cup thinly sliced red onion
¼ cup fresh basil leaves

⅓ cup extra-virgin olive oil
¼ cup balsamic vinegar
1 tablespoon freshly squeezed lemon juice
½ tablespoon raw honey
Dash salt
Freshly ground black pepper, to taste

1. In a large bowl, gently combine the greens, peaches, cherries, nectarines, pecans, red onion, and basil. 2. In a small bowl, add the olive oil, vinegar, lemon juice, honey, and salt, season with pepper, and whisk to combine. 3. Pour the dressing over the salad and gently toss to combine. Serve immediately.

Per Serving
Calories: 235 | fat: 19g | protein: 2g | carbs: 16g | fiber: 3g | sugar: 9g | sodium: 87mg

Creamy Cabbage Slaw

Prep time: 20 minutes | Cook time: 0 minutes | Serves 6

1 large head green or red cabbage, sliced thinly
2 carrots, grated
1 cup cashews, soaked in water for at least 4 hours

¼ cup freshly squeezed lemon juice
½ to ¾ cup water
¾ teaspoon sea salt

1. In a large bowl, combine the cabbage and carrots. 2. Drain and rinse the cashews. 3. In a blender, process the cashews with the lemon juice, ½ cup of water, and the salt until smooth and creamy. If the dressing is too thick, add more water, 1 tablespoon at a time. 4. Pour the sauce over the vegetables and mix well. Refrigerate for at least 1 hour before serving to give the vegetables time to marinate.

Per Serving
Calories: 208 | fat: 11g | protein: 7g | carbs: 25g | fiber: 8g | sugar: 4g | sodium: 394mg

Mediterranean Chopped Salad

Prep time: 15 minutes | Cook time: 0 minutes | Serves 4

2 cups packed spinach
3 large tomatoes, diced
1 bunch radishes, sliced thinly
1 English cucumber, peeled and diced
2 scallions, sliced
2 garlic cloves, minced
1 tablespoon chopped fresh mint
1 tablespoon chopped fresh parsley

1 cup unsweetened plain almond yogurt
¼ cup extra-virgin olive oil
3 tablespoons freshly squeezed lemon juice
1 tablespoon apple cider vinegar
1 teaspoon sea salt
¼ teaspoon freshly ground black pepper
1 tablespoon sumac

1. In a large bowl, combine the spinach, tomatoes, radishes, cucumber, scallions, garlic, mint, parsley, yogurt, olive oil, lemon juice, cider vinegar, salt, pepper, and sumac. Toss to combine.

Per Serving
Calories: 194 | fat: 14g | protein: 4g | carbs: 15g | fiber: 5g | sugar: 7g | sodium: 661mg

Massaged Swiss Chard Salad with Chopped Egg

Prep time: 25 minutes | Cook time: 0 minutes | Serves 4

Dressing:

¼ cup olive oil

3 tablespoons freshly squeezed lemon juice

2 teaspoons raw honey

1 teaspoon Dijon mustard

Sea salt, to taste

Salad:

5 cups chopped Swiss chard

3 large hard-boiled eggs, peeled and chopped

1 English cucumber, diced

½ cup sliced radishes

½ cup chopped pecans

For the Dressing:

1. In a small bowl, whisk the olive oil, lemon juice, honey, and mustard. Season with salt and set it aside.

For the Salad:

1. In a large bowl, toss the Swiss chard and dressing together for about 4 minutes, or until the greens start to soften. Divide the greens evenly among four plates. 2. Top each salad with egg, cucumber, radishes, and pecans.

Per Serving

Calories: 241 | fat: 21g | protein: 7g | carbs: 9g | fiber: 2g | sugar: 5g | sodium: 163mg

Coconut Fruit Salad

Prep time: 30 minutes | Cook time: 0 minutes | Serves 4

Dressing:

¾ cup canned lite coconut milk

2 tablespoons almond butter

2 tablespoons freshly squeezed lime juice

Salad:

6 cups mixed greens

½ pineapple, peeled, cored, and diced, or 3 cups precut packaged pineapple

1 mango, peeled, pitted, and diced, or 2 cups frozen chunks, thawed

1 cup quartered fresh strawberries

1 cup (1-inch) green bean pieces

½ cup shredded unsweetened coconut

1 tablespoon chopped fresh basil

Make the Dressing:

1. In a small bowl, whisk the coconut milk, almond butter, and lime juice until smooth. Set it aside.

Make the Salad:

1. In a large bowl, toss the mixed greens with three-fourths of the dressing. Arrange the salad on four plates. 2. In the same bowl, toss the pineapple, mango, strawberries, and green beans with the remaining fourth of the dressing. 3. Top each salad with the fruit and vegetable mixture and serve garnished with the coconut and basil.

Per Serving

Calories: 311 | fat: 19g | protein: 5g | carbs: 36g | fiber: 7g | sugar: 10g | sodium: 139mg

On-The-Go Taco Salad

Prep time: 10 minutes | Cook time: 30 minutes | Serves 4

1 tablespoon extra virgin olive oil
2 skinless chicken breasts, chopped
2 carrots, sliced
½ large onion, chopped
2 teaspoons cumin seeds

½ avocado, chopped
1 juiced lime
½ cucumber, chopped
½ cup fresh spinach, washed

1. In a skillet, heat up the oil on a medium heat and then cook the chicken for 10 to 15 minutes until browned and cooked through. 2. Remove and place to one side to cool. 3. Add the carrots and onion and continue to cook for 5 to 10 minutes or until soft. 4. Add the cumin seeds in a separate pan on a high heat and toast until they're brown before crushing them in a pestle and mortar or blender. 5. Put them into the pan with the veggies and turn off the heat. 6. Add the avocado and lime juice into a food processor and blend until creamy. 7. Layer a mason or kilner jar with half of the avocado and lime mixture, then the cumin roasted veggies, and then the chicken, packing it all in. 8. Top with the cucumbers, and spinach, refrigerating for 20 minutes before serving.

Per Serving
Calories: 338 | fat: 21g | protein: 31g | carbs: 6g | fiber: 3g | sugar: 2g | sodium: 100mg

Shredded Root Vegetable Salad

Prep time: 25 minutes | Cook time: 0 minutes | Serves 4

Dressing:
¼ cup olive oil
3 tablespoons pure maple syrup
2 tablespoons apple cider vinegar
Slaw:
1 jicama, or 2 parsnips, peeled and shredded
2 carrots, shredded, or 1 cup preshredded packaged carrots
½ celeriac, peeled and shredded
¼ fennel bulb, shredded

1 teaspoon grated fresh ginger
Sea salt, to taste

5 radishes, shredded
2 scallions, white and green parts, peeled and thinly sliced
½ cup pumpkin seeds, roasted

Make the Dressing:
1. In a small bowl, whisk the olive oil, maple syrup, cider vinegar, and ginger until well blended. Season with sea salt and set it aside.
Make the Slaw:
1. In a large bowl, toss together the jicama, carrots, celeriac, fennel, radishes, and scallions. 2. Add the dressing and toss to coat. 3. Top the slaw with the pumpkin seeds and serve.
Per Serving
Calories: 343 | fat: 21g | protein: 7g | carbs: 36g | fiber: 11g | sugar: 20g | sodium: 129mg

Grapefruit-Avocado Salad

Prep time: 20 minutes | Cook time: 0 minutes | Serves 4

Dressing:
½ avocado, peeled and pitted
¼ cup freshly squeezed lemon juice
2 tablespoons raw honey
Pinch sea salt
Water, for thinning the dressing

Salad:
4 cups fresh spinach
1 Ruby Red grapefruit, peeled, sectioned, and cut into chunks
¼ cup sliced radishes
¼ cup roasted sunflower seeds
¼ cup dried cranberries

Make the Dressing: 1. In a blender, combine the avocado, lemon juice, honey, and sea salt. Pulse until very smooth. 2. Add enough water to reach your desired consistency and set the dressing aside.
Make the Salad: 1. In a large bowl toss the spinach with half the dressing. Divide the dressed spinach among four plates. 2. Top each with grapefruit, radishes, sunflower seeds, and cranberries. 3. Drizzle the remaining half of the dressing over the salads and serve.

Per Serving
Calories: 126 | fat: 7g | protein: 2g | carbs: 16g | fiber: 3g | sugar: 9g | sodium: 29mg

Cumin and mango chicken salad

Prep time: 15 minutes | Cook time: 15 minutes | Serves 2

2 free range skinless chicken breasts
1 teaspoon oregano, finely chopped
1 garlic clove, minced
1 teaspoon chili flakes
1 teaspoon cumin
1 teaspoon turmeric
1 tablespoon extra virgin olive oil
1 lime, juiced
1 cup mango, cubed
½ iceberg, romaine lettuce or similar, sliced

1. In a bowl mix oil, garlic, herbs and spices with the lime juice. 2. Add the chicken and marinate for at least 30 minutes up to overnight. 3. When ready to serve, preheat the broiler to a medium high heat. 4. Add the chicken to a lightly greased baking tray and broil for 10 to 12 minutes or until cooked through. 5. Combine the lettuce with the mango in a serving bowl. 6. Once the chicken is cooked, serve immediately on top of the mango and lettuce.

Per Serving
Calories: 285 | fat: 13g | protein: 25g | carbs: 21g | fiber: 4g | sugar: 15g | sodium: 417mg

Pear-Walnut Salad

Prep time: 10 minutes | Cook time: 0 minutes | Serves 4

4 pears, peeled, cored, and chopped
¼ cup walnuts, chopped
2 tablespoons raw honey
2 tablespoons balsamic vinegar
2 tablespoons extra-virgin olive oil

1. In a medium bowl, combine the pears and walnuts. 2. In a small bowl, whisk the honey, balsamic vinegar, and olive oil. Toss with the pears and walnuts.

Per Serving
Calories: 263 | fat: 12g | protein: 3g | carbs: 41g | fiber: 7g | sugar: 29g | sodium: 3mg

Wild Rice Salad with Mushrooms

Prep time: 15 minutes | Cook time: 15 minutes | Serves 8

3 cups cooked wild rice
2 tablespoons ghee
1 small sweet onion, diced
3 garlic cloves, minced
2 cups cremini mushrooms, sliced
½ cup vegetable broth
½ teaspoon dried thyme
½ teaspoon salt

1. Place the rice in a large bowl and set aside. 2. In a medium saucepan over medium heat, melt the ghee. Add the onion and garlic, and cook for 5 minutes, stirring frequently. 3. Stir in the mushrooms, broth, thyme, and salt. Continue cooking for 7 to 10 minutes until the mushrooms are tender and the broth has reduced by about half. 4. Add the mushroom mixture to the rice and stir well. Serve immediately.

Per Serving
Calories: 143 | fat: 4g | protein: 5g | carbs: 22g | fiber: 2g | sugar: 3g | sodium: 186mg

Massaged Kale Salad

Prep time: 15 minutes | Cook time: 0 minutes | Serves 4

2 bunches Lacinato kale, stemmed and torn into bite-size pieces
3 scallions, sliced
1 avocado, diced
¼ cup shelled sunflower seeds
2 tablespoons freshly squeezed lemon juice
3 tablespoons extra-virgin olive oil
½ teaspoon salt
Freshly ground black pepper, to taste
¼ cup pomegranate seeds

1. In a large bowl, combine the kale, scallions, avocado, sunflower seeds, lemon juice, olive oil, and salt, and season with pepper. 2. With your hands, massage the salad ingredients for about 5 minutes until the kale begins to soften and the avocado is creamed into the other ingredients. 3. Mix the pomegranate seeds into the salad and serve immediately.

Per Serving
Calories: 249 | fat: 21g | protein: 6g | carbs: 14g | fiber: 6g | sugar: 3g | sodium: 301mg

Carrot and Raisin Salad

Prep time: 12 minutes | Cook time: 0 minutes | Serves 6

4 cups shredded carrots
1 cup raisins, chopped
¾ cup sunflower seeds
¼ cup maple syrup, plus additional as needed
¼ cup freshly squeezed lemon juice, plus additional as needed

1. In a large bowl, mix together the carrots, raisins, and sunflower seeds. 2. Stir in the maple syrup and lemon juice. 3. Taste, and add more lemon juice or maple syrup if necessary.

Per Serving
Calories: 173 | fat: 3g | protein: 3g | carbs: 37g | fiber: 3g | sugar: 26g | sodium: 57mg

Chapter 8 Desserts

108 **Lime Sorbet** 72
109 **Strawberry Jam Thumbprint Cookies** 72
110 **Sweet Ginger Pudding** 72
111 **Cherry Ice Cream** 73
112 **Honeyed Apple Cinnamon Compote** 73
113 **Chocolate-Coconut Brownies** 73
114 **Green Tea–Poached Pears** 74
115 **Spiced Savoury Pumpkin Pancakes** 74
116 **Chai Spice Baked Apples** 74
117 **Berry-Rhubarb Cobbler** 75
118 **Gluten-Free Oat and Fruit Bars** 75
119 **Coconut-Blueberry Popsicles** 77
120 **Maple-Glazed Pears with Hazelnuts** 77
121 **Maple Carrot Cake** 77
122 **Baked Fruit and Nut Pudding** 78
123 **Cranberry and Nut Slices** 78
124 **Blueberry Crisp** 78
125 **Melon with Berry-Yogurt Sauce** 79
126 **Dark Chocolate Mousse with Fruits** 79

Lime Sorbet

Prep time: 10 minutes | Cook time: 0 minutes | Serves 4

1 cup water
½ cup coconut sugar
1 cup lime juice, plus grated zest from ½ lime

1. Fill a medium bowl with ice water. Combine the 1 cup water and sugar in a small saucepan. Warm over low heat until the sugar is dissolved. Remove the simple syrup from the heat, place the pan in the ice-water bath, and stir to chill rapidly. Alternatively, refrigerate the syrup until chilled, about 3 hours. (Store in an airtight container in the refrigerator for up to 2 weeks.) 2. Combine the lime juice with 1 cup of the simple syrup in a medium bowl. Whisk in the lime zest. Freeze the sorbet in an ice-cream maker according to the manufacturer's instructions. Transfer the ice cream to a freezer-safe container and place in the freezer for 3 hours to set, or store for up to 2 weeks.

Per Serving

Calories: 68 | fat: 0g | protein: 0g | carbs: 18g | fiber: 0g | sugar: 15g | sodium: 3mg

Strawberry Jam Thumbprint Cookies

Prep time: 15 minutes | Cook time: 15 minutes | Serves 6

1½ cups sunflower seeds
3 tablespoons coconut oil
¼ cup maple syrup
½ cup strawberry jam, divided

1. Preheat the oven to 350ºF (180ºC). 2. Line a baking sheet with parchment paper. 3. In a blender, food processor, or spice grinder, process the sunflower seeds into a fine meal. Transfer to a large bowl. 4. Add the coconut oil, mashing it into the sunflower meal with a spoon as if you are crumbling butter into flour. Stir in the maple syrup. Mix well. 5. Using a tablespoon measure, scoop the dough onto the prepared sheet, making 12 cookies. Gently press down on the cookies with the back of a wet spoon to flatten them. 6. With your thumb, make imprints in the center of each cookie. Fill each depression with 2 teaspoons of strawberry jam. 7. Place the sheet in the preheated oven and bake for 12 to 14 minutes. 8. Cool before eating.

Per Serving

Calories: 392 | fat: 19g | protein: 4g | carbs: 54g | fiber: 2g | sugar: 12g | sodium: 3mg

Sweet Ginger Pudding

Prep time: 10 minutes | Cook time: 50 minutes | Serves 8

½ cup coconut oil, at room temperature, plus more for greasing the baking dish
½ cup raw honey
1 banana
1 egg
2 teaspoons grated fresh ginger
1 teaspoon pure vanilla extract
2 cups almond flour
1 teaspoon baking soda
Pinch sea salt

1. Preheat the oven to 350ºF (180ºC). 2. Lightly grease an 8-by-8-inch baking dish with coconut oil and set it aside. 3. In a large bowl, beat the coconut oil, honey, banana, egg, ginger, and vanilla with a hand beater until well mixed, scraping down the sides of the bowl at least once. 4. Beat in the almond flour, baking soda, and sea salt. Spoon the batter into the prepared dish. 5. Bake for about 50 minutes, or until it is just set and lightly browned. Serve warm.

Per Serving

Calories: 343 | fat: 26g | protein: 6g | carbs: 26g | fiber: 4g | sugar: 19g | sodium: 14mg

Cherry Ice Cream

Prep time: 10 minutes | Cook time: 0 minutes | Serves 4 to 6

1 (10-ounce / 283-g) package frozen no-added-sugar cherries
3 cups unsweetened almond milk
1 teaspoon vanilla extract
½ teaspoon almond extract

1. In a blender or food processor, combine the cherries, almond milk, vanilla extract, and almond extract. Process until mostly smooth; a few chunks of cherries are fine. 2. Pour the mixture into a container with an airtight lid. Freeze thoroughly before serving.

Per Serving

Calories: 82 | fat: 2g | protein: 1g | carbs: 14g | fiber: 2g | sugar: 12g | sodium: 121mg

Honeyed Apple Cinnamon Compote

Prep time: 15 minutes | Cook time: 10 minutes | Serves 4

6 apples, peeled, cored, and chopped
¼ cup apple juice
¼ cup honey
1 teaspoon ground cinnamon
pinch sea salt

1. In a large pot over medium-high heat, combine the apples, apple juice, honey, cinnamon, and salt. Simmer for about 10 minutes, stirring occasionally, until the apples are still quite chunky but also saucy.

Per Serving

Calories: 247 | fat: 1g | protein: 1g | carbs: 66g | fiber: 9g | sugar: 44g | sodium: 63mg

Chocolate-Coconut Brownies

Prep time: 15 minutes | Cook time: 35 minutes | Makes 16 brownies

½ cup gluten-free flour, such as Cup4Cup or Bob's Red Mill
¼ cup unsweetened alkalized cocoa powder
½ teaspoon sea salt
4 ounces (113 g) semisweet chocolate, coarsely chopped
¾ cup unrefined coconut oil
1 cup coconut sugar
4 eggs
1 teaspoon vanilla
4 ounces (113 g) semisweet chocolate chips (optional)

1. Preheat the oven to 350°F (180°C). Grease a 9-by-9-inch baking pan and line with parchment paper. 2. Combine the flour, cocoa powder, and salt in a medium bowl. Set aside. 3. In a double boiler or microwave, melt the chopped chocolate and coconut oil. Let cool slightly. Add the sugar, eggs, and vanilla, whisking until well combined. Whisk in the flour mixture. Fold in the chocolate chips (if using). Pour into the prepared pan. Bake until a toothpick inserted in the center of the brownies comes out clean, 20 to 25 minutes. This will yield a somewhat gooey brownie. Continue to bake for 5 to 10 minutes if you prefer a drier brownie. 4. Let the brownies cool completely, then cut into squares. Store in an airtight container at room temperature for up to 3 days.

Per Serving

Calories: 382 | fat: 29g | protein: 6g | carbs: 28g | fiber: 4g | sugar: 15g | sodium: 180mg

Green Tea-Poached Pears

Prep time: 5 minutes | Cook time: 15 minutes | Serves 4

4 pears, peeled, cored, and quartered lengthwise
2 cups strongly brewed green tea
¼ cup honey
1 tablespoon grated fresh ginger

1. In a large pot over medium-high heat, combine the pears, tea, honey, and ginger. Bring to a simmer. Reduce the heat to medium-low, cover, and simmer for about 15 minutes until the pears soften. Serve the pears with the poaching liquid spooned over the top.

Per Serving

Calories: 190 | fat: 1g | protein: 1g | carbs: 50g | fiber: 7g | sugar: 36g | sodium: 4mg

Spiced Savoury Pumpkin Pancakes

Prep time: 10 minutes | Cook time: 10 minutes | Serves 4

Flesh from ½ deseeded pumpkin
4 eggs
3 egg whites
Sprinkle of black pepper
½ teaspoon gluten-free baking soda
2 tablespoons coconut oil
1 tablespoon raw honey
1 handful pecan nuts

1. In a blender or food processor, blend the pumpkin flesh together with some water to form a smooth pulp. 2. Now add the eggs, freshly ground pepper, 1 tablespoon of coconut oil, and a tiny pinch of baking soda to the pumpkin mix and blend until smooth. 3. Heat a large pan on a medium heat with the other 1 tablespoon of coconut oil. 4. Pour individual rounded pancakes into your pan (go easy at first and pour your mixture into little circles, keep pouring whilst tilting the pan until you have a pancake to your desired shape). 5. Cook for 3 minutes then flip. 6. Plate and serve with pecan nuts and honey.

Per Serving

Calories: 252 | fat: 20g | protein: 10g | carbs: 11g | fiber: 2g | sugar: 7g | sodium: 262mg

Chai Spice Baked Apples

Prep time: 15 minutes | Cook time: 2 to 3 hours | Makes 5 apples

5 apples
½ cup water
½ cup crushed pecans (optional)
¼ cup melted coconut oil
1 teaspoon ground cinnamon
½ teaspoon ground ginger
¼ teaspoon ground cardamom
¼ teaspoon ground cloves

1. Core each apple, and peel off a thin strip from the top of each. 2. Add the water to the slow cooker. Gently place each apple upright along the bottom. 3. In a small bowl, stir together the pecans (if using), coconut oil, cinnamon, ginger, cardamom, and cloves. Drizzle the mixture over the tops of the apples. 4. Cover the cooker and set to high. Cook for 2 to 3 hours, until the apples soften, and serve.

Per Serving

Calories: 217 | fat: 12g | protein: 0g | carbs: 30g | fiber: 6g | sugar: 20g | sodium: 0mg

Berry-Rhubarb Cobbler

Prep time: 15 minutes | Cook time: 35 minutes | Serves 8

Cobbler:

Coconut oil, for greasing the baking dish

2 cups fresh blueberries

1 cup fresh raspberries

1 cup sliced (½-inch) rhubarb pieces

Topping:

1 cup almond flour

½ cup shredded unsweetened coconut

1 tablespoon arrowroot powder

¼ cup unsweetened apple juice

¼ cup raw honey

1 tablespoon arrowroot powder

½ cup coconut oil

¼ cup raw honey

Make the Cobbler:

1. Preheat the oven to 350°F (180°C). 2. Lightly grease a 9-by-9-inch baking dish with coconut oil and set it aside. 3. In a large bowl, toss together the blueberries, raspberries, rhubarb, apple juice, honey, and arrowroot powder until combined. Transfer the fruit mixture to the prepared dish and spread it out evenly.

Make the Topping:

1. In a small bowl, stir together the almond flour, coconut, and arrowroot powder until well mixed. 2. Add the coconut oil and honey. With a fork, mix until coarse crumbs form. Spread the topping on top of the fruit in the baking dish. 3. Bake the crumble for about 35 minutes, or until bubbly and golden.

Per Serving

Calories: 304 | fat: 22g | protein: 3g | carbs: 30g | fiber: 4g | sugar: 23g | sodium: 3mg

Gluten-Free Oat and Fruit Bars

Prep time: 15 minutes | Cook time: 40 to 45 minutes | Makes 16 bars

Cooking spray

½ cup maple syrup

½ cup almond or sunflower butter

2 medium ripe bananas, mashed

⅓ cup dried cranberries

1½ cups old-fashioned rolled oats

½ cup shredded coconut

¼ cup oat flour

¼ cup ground flaxseed

1 teaspoon vanilla extract

½ teaspoon ground cinnamon

¼ teaspoon ground cloves

1. Preheat the oven to 400°F (205°C). 2. Line an 8-by-8-inch square pan with parchment paper or aluminum foil, and coat the lined pan with cooking spray. 3. In a medium bowl, combine the maple syrup, almond butter, and bananas. Mix until well blended. 4. Add the cranberries, oats, coconut, oat flour, flaxseed, vanilla, cinnamon, and cloves. Mix well. 5. Spoon the mixture into the prepared pan; the mixture will be thick and sticky. Use an oiled spatula to spread the mixture evenly. 6. Place the pan in the preheated oven and bake for 40 to 45 minutes, or until the top is dry and a toothpick inserted in the middle comes out clean. Cool completely before cutting into bars.

Per Serving

Calories: 144 | fat: 7g | protein: 3g | carbs: 19g | fiber: 2g | sugar: 8g | sodium: 3mg

Coconut-Blueberry Popsicles

Prep time: 15 minutes | Cook time: 0 minutes | Serves 6

1 cup fresh blueberries
1½ cups coconut milk
¼ cup maple syrup

¼ teaspoon cinnamon
⅛ teaspoon salt

1. In a small bowl, roughly mash the blueberries. 2. Divide the blueberry mixture among 6 ice pop molds. 3. In a medium bowl, mix together the coconut milk, maple syrup, cinnamon, and salt. 4. Pour the coconut milk mixture into the ice pop molds over the blueberries. 5. Freeze for at least 2 hours, or until solid.

Per Serving

Calories: 186 | fat: 14g | protein: 2g | carbs: 16g | fiber: 2g | sugar: 12g | sodium: 37mg

Maple-Glazed Pears with Hazelnuts

Prep time: 10 minutes | Cook time: 20 minutes | Serves 4

4 pears, peeled, cored, and quartered lengthwise
1 cup apple juice
½ cup pure maple syrup

1 tablespoon grated fresh ginger
¼ cup chopped hazelnuts

1. In a large pot over medium-high heat, combine the pears and apple juice. Bring to a simmer and reduce the heat to medium-low. Cover and simmer for 15 to 20 minutes until the pears soften. 2. While the pears poach, in a small saucepan over medium-high heat, combine the maple syrup and ginger. Bring to a simmer, stirring. Remove the pan from the heat and let the syrup rest. 3. Using a slotted spoon, remove the pears from the poaching liquid and brush with the maple syrup. Serve topped with the hazelnuts.

Per Serving

Calories: 286 | fat: 3g | protein: 2g | carbs: 67g | fiber: 7g | sugar: 50g | sodium: 9mg

Maple Carrot Cake

Prep time: 15 minutes | Cook time: 45 minutes | Serves 12

½ cup coconut oil, at room temperature, plus more for greasing the baking dish
¼ cup pure maple syrup
2 teaspoons pure vanilla extract
6 eggs
½ cup coconut flour
1 teaspoon baking soda

1 teaspoon baking powder
1 teaspoon ground cinnamon
½ teaspoon ground nutmeg
⅛ teaspoon sea salt
3 cups finely grated carrots
½ cup chopped pecans

1. Preheat the oven to 350ºF (180ºC). 2. Lightly grease a 9-by-13-inch baking dish with coconut oil and set it aside. 3. In a large bowl, whisk the ½ cup of coconut oil, maple syrup, and vanilla until blended. 4. One at a time, whisk in the eggs, beating well after each addition. 5. In a medium bowl, stir together the coconut flour, baking soda, baking powder, cinnamon, nutmeg, and sea salt. Add the dry ingredients to the wet ingredients, and stir until just combined. 6. Stir in the carrots and pecans until mixed. Spoon the batter into the prepared dish. 7. Bake for about 45 minutes, or until a toothpick inserted in the center comes out clean. 8. Cool the cake on a wire rack and serve.

Per Serving

Calories: 254 | fat: 21g | protein: 5g | carbs: 13g | fiber: 2g | sugar: 5g | sodium: 73mg

Baked Fruit and Nut Pudding

Prep time: 10 minutes | Cook time: 1 hour | Serves 4

15 apricots
10 prunes
6 free range eggs
3 cups water

1 cup raw pecans or walnuts
2 tablespoons pure vanilla extract
2 broken cinnamon sticks

1. Preheat oven to 350°F (180°C). 2. In a large saucepan, boil the water on a high heat and then add the apricots, prunes, and cinnamon sticks before turning down the heat and simmering for 30 minutes. 3. Allow to cool. 4. Remove the cinnamon sticks and blend mixture, adding in the eggs and vanilla until smooth. 5. Add mixture to a glass oven dish and top with the nuts. 6. Oven bake for 30 minutes. 7. Cool and serve.

Per Serving

Calories: 353 | fat: 20g | protein: 14g | carbs: 31g | fiber: 6g | sugar: 14g | sodium: 101mg

Cranberry and Nut Slices

Prep time: 10 minutes | Cook time: 0 minutes | Serves 2

1 tablespoon dried dates, diced
1 tablespoon dried cranberries

1 tablespoon coconut flakes
1 tablespoon ground walnuts or pecans

1. Mix all of the ingredients in a bowl. 2. Use your hands to shape the mixture into a ball. 3. Lay out tin foil and then flatten and roll the mixture with the palms of your hands to form a cylinder shape. 4. Roll and wrap in the tinfoil and then leave in the fridge for 30 minutes until it hardens before slicing into disk shape slices. 5. Serve with fresh fruit.

Per Serving

Calories: 96 | fat: 3g | protein: 2g | carbs: 18g | fiber: 3g | sugar: 13g | sodium: 8mg

Blueberry Crisp

Prep time: 15 minutes | Cook time: 20 minutes | Serves 4

½ cup coconut oil, melted, plus additional for brushing
1 quart fresh blueberries
¼ cup maple syrup
Juice of ½ lemon
2 teaspoons lemon zest

1 cup gluten-free rolled oats
½ teaspoon ground cinnamon
½ cup chopped pecans
Pinch salt

1. Preheat the oven to 350°F (180°C). 2. Brush a shallow baking dish with melted coconut oil. Stir together the blueberries, maple syrup, lemon juice, and lemon zest in the dish. 3. In a small bowl, combine the oats, ½ cup of melted coconut oil, cinnamon, pecans, and salt. Mix the ingredients well to evenly distribute the coconut oil. Sprinkle the oat mixture over the berries. 4. Place the dish in the preheated oven and bake for 20 minutes, or until the oats are lightly browned.

Per Serving

Calories: 497 | fat: 33g | protein: 5g | carbs: 51g | fiber: 7g | sugar: 26g | sodium: 42mg

Melon with Berry-Yogurt Sauce

Prep time: 15 minutes | Cook time: 0 minutes | Serves 6

1 cantaloupe, peeled and sliced
1 pint fresh raspberries
½ teaspoon vanilla extract

1 cup plain coconut or almond yogurt
½ cup toasted coconut

1. Arrange the melon slices on a serving plate. 2. In a small bowl, mash the berries with the vanilla. Add the yogurt and stir until just mixed. 3. Spoon the berry-yogurt mixture over the melon slices and sprinkle with the coconut.

Per Serving
Calories: 76 | fat: 4g | protein: 1g | carbs: 11g | fiber: 6g | sugar: 5g | sodium: 37mg

Dark Chocolate Mousse with Fruits

Prep time: 10 minutes | Cook time: 5 minutes | Serves 2

1 cup of strawberries, sliced
¼ cup of free range egg whites
4 squares dark cooking chocolate

1 small banana, sliced
½ cup blueberries
2 tablespoons of water

1. Melt the dark chocolate over a bowl of boiling water on a low heat on the stove. 2. Add the water and egg whites to the melted chocolate and mix well to reach a thick consistency. 3. Spoon the batter out onto a small plate. 4. Put in the freezer for half an hour. 5. Garnish with the strawberries, banana and blueberries to serve.

Per Serving
Calories: 256 | fat: 11g | protein: 7g | carbs: 34g | fiber: 6g | sugar: 19g | sodium: 59mg

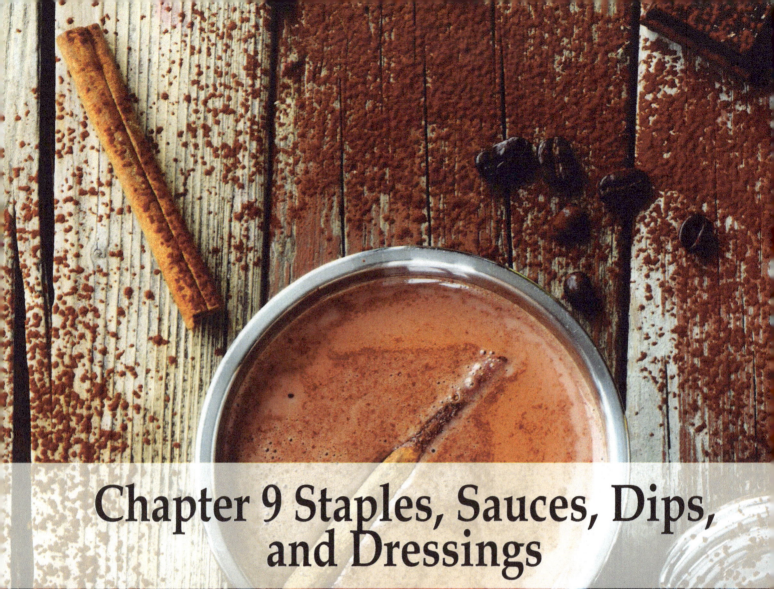

Chapter 9 Staples, Sauces, Dips, and Dressings

127	**Fiesta Guacamole**	82
128	**Pie Crust**	82
129	**Peach Butter**	82
130	**Avocado-Dill Sauce**	83
131	**Homemade Mayo**	83
132	**Addictive Multi-Purpose Cream Sauce**	83
133	**Beans**	85
134	**Vegan Buffalo Dip**	85
135	**Almond-Hazelnut Milk**	85
136	**Lemon-Ginger Honey**	86
137	**Garlic-Lemon Vinaigrette**	86

Fiesta Guacamole

Prep time: 15 minutes | Cook time: 0 minutes | Makes 3 cups

3 medium Hass avocados, halved, pitted, and peeled
3 small radishes, sliced
3 large strawberries, diced
3 cloves garlic, minced
1 green onion, sliced
½ bunch fresh cilantro (about 1½ ounces / 43 g), minced
Juice of 2 lemons
2 teaspoons fine Himalayan salt
1 tablespoon extra-virgin olive oil

1. Place all the ingredients in a large bowl. Use a whisk or pestle to mix and mash them together until you have a chunky guacamole. 2. If it's not all going to be consumed right away, transfer it to an airtight container, drizzle olive oil on it, set a sheet of plastic wrap on the top so that it sticks directly to the guacamole—this will help keep the avocado from turning brown—and then put the lid on. Store in the fridge until ready to enjoy, but no more than 4 days.

Per Serving
Calories: 215 | fat: 18g | protein: 4g | carbs: 5g | fiber: 3g | sugar: 1g | sodium: 354mg

Pie Crust

Prep time: 20 minutes | Cook time: 15 minutes | Makes 1 pie crust

4 large eggs
½ cup melted coconut oil
¼ teaspoon fine Himalayan salt
1 teaspoon coconut sugar (optional)
⅓ cup plus 1 tablespoon coconut flour

1. Preheat the oven to 400ºF (205ºC). 2. In a small bowl, whisk the eggs as you slowly pour in the coconut oil—it will become creamy. Then add the salt and sugar (if using) and stir to combine. Add the coconut flour and fold until a dough forms. 3. Transfer the dough to an 8-inch pie pan and use your fingers to gently press it into the dish, bringing it 1 inch up the sides. Pie crust is all about patience and finesse. Work slowly; aim to make the thickness even throughout, and make sure the 1-inch crust on the sides is level all around. 4. Use a fork to poke a few holes in the bottom of the crust. Bake for 15 minutes, or until golden with browned edges. 5. Use to make a pie right away, or wrap it up in the pie pan and freeze for up to 30 days. To thaw and heat, bake in a preheated 400ºF (205ºC) oven for 15 minutes.

Per Serving
Calories: 312 | fat: 32g | protein: 7g | carbs: 1g | fiber: 0g | sugar: 1g | sodium: 248mg

Peach Butter

Prep time: 10 minutes | Cook time: 3 hours 30 minutes | Makes 2 cups

8 peaches (about 3 pounds / 1.4 kg), peeled, pitted, and chopped, or about 6 cups frozen, sliced peaches
Water, for cooking
¼ cup raw honey

1. In a large saucepan over high heat, combine the peaches with enough water to cover the fruit by about 1 inch. Bring the liquid to a boil. 2. Reduce the heat to low and simmer for about 3 hours, stirring frequently until the mixture resembles a thick applesauce. 3. Stir in the honey. Simmer for about 30 minutes until the mixture starts to caramelize. Remove the peach butter from the heat and let it cool for 30 minutes. 4. Spoon the mixture into a container and cool completely before covering. Keep refrigerated for up to 2 weeks.

Per Serving
Calories: 46 | fat: 0g | protein: 1g | carbs: 11g | fiber: 1g | sugar: 9g | sodium: 0mg

Avocado-Dill Sauce

Prep time: 15 minutes | Cook time: 0 minutes | Makes about 1 cup

1 large, ripe avocado, peeled and pitted
2 teaspoons fresh dill
2 teaspoons freshly squeezed lemon juice

½ teaspoon sea salt
Dash red pepper flakes
Chopped veggies, for serving (if desired)

1. In a blender, combine the avocado, dill, lemon juice, salt, and red pepper flakes. Pulse until smooth. If the sauce is too thick, add water to thin as needed. Serve with chopped veggies (if using).

Per Serving
Calories: 301 | fat: 27g | protein: 4g | carbs: 19g | fiber: 12g | sugar: 2g | sodium: 1077mg

Homemade Mayo

Prep time: 5 minutes | Cook time: 0 minutes | Makes 1 cup

3 tablespoons coconut vinegar
1 teaspoon dried thyme leaves
½ teaspoon granulated garlic
½ teaspoon dry mustard

½ teaspoon fine Himalayan salt
3 large egg yolks
1 cup avocado oil

1. Place the vinegar and seasonings in a 16-ounce (454-g) measuring cup or quart-sized mason jar. Gently add the egg yolks and then the avocado oil. 2. Insert the immersion blender into the mixture, turn it on high, and move it up and down slightly until the mix is completely emulsified. Use a spatula to scrape all of the mayonnaise off of the blender and then to transfer the mayonnaise to a jar or other container with a tight-fitting lid. 3. Store in the refrigerator for up to 10 days, and always use clean utensils when serving.

Per Serving
Calories: 262 | fat: 19g | protein: 1g | carbs: 0g | fiber: 0g | sugar: 0g | sodium: 152mg

Addictive Multi-Purpose Cream Sauce

Prep time: 10 minutes | Cook time: 12 minutes | Makes 3½ cups

3 cups cubed butternut squash
½ cup cashews, soaked in water for at least 4 hours, drained

½ cup water, plus additional for cooking and thinning
1 teaspoon salt, plus additional as needed

1. Fill a large pot with 2 inches of water and insert a steamer basket. Bring to a boil over high heat. 2. Add the butternut squash to the basket. Cover and steam for 10 to 12 minutes, or until tender. 3. Remove from the heat and cool slightly. 4. Transfer the squash to a blender. Add the cashews, ½ cup of water, and salt. Blend until smooth and creamy. Depending on the consistency, add more water to thin if necessary. 5. Taste, and adjust the seasoning if necessary.

Per Serving
Calories: 73 | fat: 5g | protein: 2g | carbs: 8g | fiber: 1g | sugar: 1g | sodium: 335mg

Beans

Prep time: 30 minutes | Cook time: 1 hour | Makes 2½ cups

8 ounces (227 g) dried beans
Filtered water, for soaking and cooking
Pinch salt

Seasonings, such as bay leaves, garlic, onion, cumin (optional)

1. In a large glass bowl, cover the beans with water. Add the salt and let soak on the counter, covered, overnight. 2. Drain the beans and rinse well. Transfer to a large pot and add any seasonings you like (if using). 3. Cover the beans with 1 to 2 inches of water, place the pot over high heat, and bring to a boil. Reduce heat to low and simmer for 1 hour. 4. Check the beans for doneness; some varieties require longer cooking times. Continue to simmer, if needed, and check every 10 minutes until done. Use immediately in soups or chilis, or refrigerate in an airtight container for up to 1 week. Cooked beans can also be frozen for up to 3 months.

Per Serving
Calories: 153 | fat: 1g | protein: 10g | carbs: 28g | fiber: 7g | sugar: 0g | sodium: 42mg

Vegan Buffalo Dip

Prep time: 15 minutes | Cook time: 5 to 6 hours | Serves 4 to 6

1 pound (454 g) cauliflower, chopped
1¼ cups raw cashews, soaked in water overnight, drained
¾ cup hot sauce
½ cup water
1 tablespoon freshly squeezed lemon juice

1 teaspoon garlic powder
½ teaspoon paprika
Sea salt, to taste
Freshly ground black pepper, to taste
Chopped veggies, for serving (optional)

1. In your slow cooker, combine the cauliflower, cashews, hot sauce, water, lemon juice, garlic powder, and paprika. Season with salt and pepper. 2. Cover the cooker and set to low. Cook for 5 to 6 hours. 3. Transfer the mixture to a blender or food processor. Pulse until the desired consistency is reached. Serve with chopped veggies (if using).

Per Serving
Calories: 302 | fat: 18g | protein: 9g | carbs: 26g | fiber: 6g | sugar: 14g | sodium:574 mg

Almond-Hazelnut Milk

Prep time: 15 minutes | Cook time: 0 minutes | Makes about 4 cups

½ cup soaked raw hazelnuts, drained
½ cup soaked raw almonds, drained
4 cups filtered water

1 teaspoon raw honey (optional)
¼ teaspoon vanilla extract (optional)

1. In a colander, combine the hazelnuts and almonds and give them a good rinse. Transfer to a blender and add the water. Blend at high speed for 30 seconds. 2. Place a nut milk bag or other mesh-like material over a large bowl and carefully pour the nut mixture into it. 3. Pick up the top of the bag and strain the liquid into the bowl, squeezing the pulp to remove as much liquid as possible. 4. Using a funnel, transfer the nut milk to a sealable bottle. Add the honey (if using) and vanilla (if using). Seal the bottle and shake well. Refrigerate for up to 4 days.

Per Serving
Calories: 85 | fat: 5g | protein: 2g | carbs: 10g | fiber: 1g | sugar: 3g | sodium: 5mg

Lemon-Ginger Honey

Prep time: 10 minutes | Cook time: 0 minutes | Makes about 1 cup

1 cup water
¼ cup fresh lemon juice
2 tablespoons honey
2 teaspoons grated fresh ginger root

1. Combine all the ingredients in an airtight jar and shake until the honey is dissolved. 2. Refrigerate for 24 hours before using so the ginger can permeate the mixture. 3. Store in the refrigerator up to a week.

Per Serving
Calories: 20 | fat: 0g | protein: 0g | carbs: 5g | fiber: 0g | sugar: 4g | sodium: 0mg

Garlic-Lemon Vinaigrette

Prep time: 10 minutes | Cook time: 0 minutes | Makes ¾ cup

1 garlic clove
Kosher salt, to taste
1 tablespoon plus 1 teaspoon Dijon mustard, plus more as needed
¼ cup lemon juice, plus more as needed
½ cup organic extra-virgin olive oil or canola oil
Freshly ground black pepper

1. Place the garlic on a cutting board and smash with the flat side of a chef's knife. Sprinkle with ¼ teaspoon salt. Use the knife to mince the garlic, then scrape it into a small pile and use the side of the knife to press the garlic and salt together. Repeat the process until the garlic and salt form a paste. 2. Place the garlic paste in a small bowl and add the mustard. Whisk in the lemon juice, then slowly whisk in the olive oil to combine. Add a few grindings of pepper. Taste, adding more salt, lemon juice, or Dijon as desired. 3. Store in an airtight glass container in the refrigerator for up to 1 week. Whisk again just before serving to re-emulsify.

Per Serving
Calories: 164 | fat: 18g | protein: 0g | carbs: 1g | fiber: 0g | sugar: 0g | sodium: 417mg

Chapter 10 Snacks and Appetizers

138 Curry-Spiced Nut Mix with Maple and Black Pepper   89

139 Chickpea Paste   89

140 Garlicky Roasted Chickpeas   89

141 Fast and Fresh Granola Trail Mix   90

142 Plantain Chips   90

143 Spicy Two-Bean Dip   90

144 Spinach and Kale Breaded Balls   92

145 Mashed Avocado with Jicama Slices   92

146 Crispy Thin Flatbread   92

147 Cashew "Hummus" Dip   93

148 Amazing Apricot Bites   93

149 Simplest Guacamole   93

150 Turmeric-Almond Smoothie   93

Curry-Spiced Nut Mix with Maple and Black Pepper

Prep time: 10 minutes | Cook time: 35 minutes | Makes 2 cups

1 cup raw cashew pieces
½ cup raw macadamia nuts, roughly chopped
½ cup raw pumpkin seeds
1 tablespoon fresh-pressed coconut oil
2 teaspoons maple syrup

2 teaspoons curry powder
½ teaspoon kosher salt
¼ teaspoon freshly ground black pepper
Pinch of cayenne pepper

1. Preheat the oven to 300ºF (150ºC). Line a baking sheet with parchment paper. 2. Combine the cashews, macadamias, and pumpkin seeds in a large bowl. 3. In a medium saucepan over low heat, melt the coconut oil with the maple syrup, about 1 minute. Remove from the heat and pour over the nut mixture. Add the curry powder, salt, black pepper, and cayenne pepper and stir well to coat. Spread the mixture on the prepared baking sheet. 4. Bake, stirring once, until the nuts are light brown, 30 to 35 minutes. Let cool on the baking sheet. 5. Store in an airtight container at room temperature for up to 3 days.

Per Serving
Calories: 425 | fat: 34g | protein: 11g | carbs: 25g | fiber: 6g | sugar: 5g | sodium: 300mg

Chickpea Paste

Prep time: 15 minutes | Cook time: 0 minutes | Makes about 2 cups

1 (15-ounce / 425-g) can chickpeas, drained and rinsed
¼ cup extra-virgin olive oil
¼ cup fresh lemon juice
¼ cup minced onion

1 garlic clove, minced
1 teaspoon sea salt
½ teaspoon ground cumin

1. In a medium bowl, use a potato masher to mash the chickpeas until they are mostly broken up. 2. Add the olive oil, lemon juice, onion, garlic, salt, cumin, and and continue mashing until you have a slightly chunky paste. Let sit for 30 minutes at room temperature for the flavors to develop, then serve.

Per Serving
Calories: 110 | fat: 8g | protein: 3g | carbs: 10g | fiber: 2g | sugar: 2g | sodium: 290mg

Garlicky Roasted Chickpeas

Prep time: 5 minutes | Cook time: 20 minutes | Makes 4 cups

4 cups cooked (or canned) chickpeas, rinsed, drained, and thoroughly dried with paper towels (be careful not to crush them)
2 tablespoons extra-virgin olive oil

1 teaspoon salt
1 teaspoon garlic powder
Freshly ground black pepper, to taste

1. Preheat the oven to 400ºF (205ºC). 2. Spread the chickpeas evenly on a rimmed baking sheet and coat them with the olive oil. 3. Bake for 20 minutes, stirring halfway through. 4. Transfer the hot chickpeas to a large bowl. Toss with the salt and garlic powder; season with pepper. Store leftovers in a sealed container or bag at room temperature; they'll remain crispy for 1 to 2 days.

Per Serving
Calories: 150 | fat: 5g | protein: 6g | carbs: 21g | fiber: 6g | sugar: 3g | sodium: 148mg

Fast and Fresh Granola Trail Mix

Prep time: 5 minutes | Cook time: 20 minutes | Serves 2

1 cup toasted almonds
1 tablespoon raw honey
½ cup cherries
1 cup granola

1. Preheat oven to 350ºF (180ºC). 2. Spread the almonds across a baking sheet. 3. Bake for five minutes and then add cherries and granola and toss. 4. Drizzle honey on top and toss again to coat before baking in oven for 10 to 15 minutes. 5. Remove to cool and serve.

Per Serving
Calories: 539 | fat: 27g | protein: 18g | carbs: 58g | fiber: 10g | sugar: 16g | sodium: 11mg

Plantain Chips

Prep time: 10 minutes | Cook time: 20 minutes | Makes 2 cups

2 pounds (907 g) plantains, peeled and sliced thinly on the diagonal
¼ cup olive oil
½ teaspoon smoked paprika
½ teaspoon kosher salt

1. Preheat the oven to 375ºF (190ºC). Line two baking sheets with parchment paper. 2. Lay the plantain slices in a single layer on the prepared baking sheets. Brush the tops of the slices with half of the olive oil, then turn them over and brush the other side with oil. Sprinkle with the paprika and salt. 3. Roast for 18 to 20 minutes, turning halfway through, until the plantains are golden and crunchy. Let cool completely. 4. Store in an airtight container at room temperature for up to 3 days.

Per Serving
Calories: 397 | fat: 14g | protein: 3g | carbs: 59g | fiber: 5g | sugar: 24g | sodium: 300mg

Spicy Two-Bean Dip

Prep time: 10 minutes | Cook time: 0 minutes | Makes about 3½ cups

1 (14-ounce / 397-g) can black beans, drained and rinsed well
1 (14-ounce / 397-g) can kidney beans, drained and rinsed well
2 garlic cloves
2 cherry tomatoes
2 tablespoons filtered water
1 tablespoon apple cider vinegar
2 teaspoons raw honey
1 teaspoon freshly squeezed lime juice
¼ teaspoon ground cumin
¼ teaspoon salt
Pinch cayenne pepper
Freshly ground black pepper, to taste

1. In a food processor (or blender), combine the black beans, kidney beans, garlic, tomatoes, water, vinegar, honey, lime juice, cumin, salt, and cayenne pepper, and season with black pepper. Blend until smooth. Use a silicone spatula to scrape the sides of the processor bowl as needed. Cover and refrigerate before serving, if desired, or refrigerate for up to 5 days.

Per Serving
Calories: 166 | fat: 0g | protein: 9g | carbs: 34g | fiber: 8g | sugar: 5g | sodium: 404mg

Spinach and Kale Breaded Balls

Prep time: 15 minutes | Cook time: 30 minutes | Serves 4

2 cups frozen or fresh spinach, thawed and chopped
1 cup of frozen or fresh kale, thawed and drained
½ cup onion, finely chopped
1 garlic clove, finely chopped
3 tablespoons extra virgin olive oil
2 free range eggs, beaten
½ teaspoon ground thyme
½ teaspoon rubbed dried oregano
½ teaspoon dried rosemary
1 cup dry 100% wholegrain bread crumbs
½ teaspoon dried oregano
1 teaspoon ground black pepper

1. Preheat oven to 350ºF (180ºC). 2. Line a baking sheet with parchment paper. 3. In a bowl, mix the olive oil and eggs, adding in the spinach, garlic and onions and tossing to coat. 4. Add the rest of the ingredients, mixing to blend. 5. Use the palms of your hands to roll into 1 inch balls and arrange them onto the baking sheet. 6. Bake for 15 minutes, and then flip the balls over. 7. Continue to bake for another 15 minutes or until they're golden brown. 8. Serve and enjoy!

Per Serving
Calories: 262 | fat: 14g | protein: 10g | carbs: 26g | fiber: 4g | sugar: 3g | sodium: 289mg

Mashed Avocado with Jicama Slices

Prep time: 15 minutes | Cook time: 0 minutes | Serves 4

2 ripe avocados, pitted
1 scallion, sliced
2 tablespoons chopped fresh cilantro
½ teaspoon ground turmeric
Juice of ½ lemon
1 teaspoon salt
¼ teaspoon freshly ground black pepper
1 jicama, peeled and cut into ¼-inch-thick slices

1. In a small bowl, combine the scooped-out avocado, the scallion, cilantro, turmeric, lemon juice, salt, and pepper. Mash the ingredients together until well mixed and still slightly chunky. 2. Serve with the jicama slices.

Per Serving
Calories: 270 | fat: 20g | protein: 3g | carbs: 24g | fiber: 15g | sugar: 4g | sodium: 595mg

Crispy Thin Flatbread

Prep time: 10 minutes | Cook time: 20 minutes | Makes 2 crusts

4 large cold eggs
½ cup coconut oil, melted
½ teaspoon fine Himalayan salt
⅓ cup coconut flour, plus more if needed

1. Preheat the oven to 400ºF (205ºC). Line a baking sheet with parchment paper. 2. In a small bowl, whisk the eggs as you slowly pour in the coconut oil—it will become creamy. Then add the salt and stir to combine. Add the coconut flour and fold until a loose dough forms 3. The density of coconut flour can vary from brand to brand. If the dough does not take shape, add more flour a teaspoon at a time, waiting at least 30 seconds before adding the next teaspoon, until a pliable dough forms. 4. Separate the dough into 2 large balls. Use a spoon or spatula to spread each ball into a ¼-inch-thick, 8-inch round on the prepared baking sheet. 5. Bake for 15 to 20 minutes, until the center is firm and the edges are browned. Remove from the oven and let cool. 6. These flatbreads can be wrapped up tight and stored in the fridge for up to 4 days. To reheat, bake in a preheated 350ºF (180ºC) oven for 8 minutes.

Per Serving
Calories: 395 | fat: 35g | protein: 9g | carbs: 12g | fiber: 7g | sugar: 1g | sodium: 372mg

Cashew "Hummus" Dip

Prep time: 20 minutes | Cook time: 0 minutes | Makes about 1 cup

1 cup raw cashews, soaked in filtered water for 15 minutes and drained
2 garlic cloves
¼ cup filtered water
1 tablespoon extra-virgin olive oil
2 teaspoons coconut aminos
1 teaspoon freshly squeezed lemon juice
½ teaspoon ground ginger
¼ teaspoon salt
Pinch cayenne pepper

1. In a food processor (or blender), combine the cashews, garlic, water, olive oil, aminos, lemon juice, ginger, salt, and cayenne pepper. Blend until smooth. Use a silicone spatula to scrape down the sides of the processor bowl as needed. 2. Cover and refrigerate before serving, if desired, or refrigerate for up to 5 days.

Per Serving
Calories: 112 | fat: 8g | protein: 3g | carbs: 5g | fiber: 0g | sugar: 1g | sodium: 102mg

Amazing Apricot Bites

Prep time: 5 minutes | Cook time: 0 minutes | Serves 4

1 cup dried apricots, finely chopped
1 cup raw walnuts or pecans, finely chopped
½ cup desiccated coconut
1 tablespoon honey

1. Mix the ingredients together to form a sticky dough. 2. Shape into 8 bite size balls with the palms of your hands. 3. Cover and refrigerate for at least 2 hours to set. 4. Serve or wrap for later.

Per Serving
Calories: 334 | fat: 22g | protein: 6g | carbs: 34g | fiber: 5g | sugar: 26g | sodium: 34mg

Simplest Guacamole

Prep time: 10 minutes | Cook time: 0 minutes | Makes about 3 cups

4 medium, ripe avocados, halved and pitted
1 teaspoon garlic powder
½ teaspoon salt

1. Scoop out the avocado flesh and put it in a medium bowl. 2. Add the garlic powder and the salt. With a fork, mash the avocados until creamy. 3. Serve immediately, or cover and refrigerate for up to 2 days.

Per Serving
Calories: 358 | fat: 32g | protein: 7g | carbs: 13g | fiber: 6g | sugar: 1g | sodium: 244mg

Turmeric-Almond Smoothie

Prep time: 10 minutes | Cook time: 0 minutes | Serves 2

1 pear, cored and quartered
2 cups baby spinach
¼ avocado
1 cup silken tofu
1 teaspoon ground turmeric or 1 thin slice peeled turmeric root
½ cup unsweetened almond milk
2 tablespoons honey (optional)
1 cup ice

1. In a blender, combine all the ingredients and blend until smooth. Divide between two glasses, and serve.

Per Serving
Calories: 270 | fat: 11g | protein: 10g | carbs: 38g | fiber: 6g | sugar: 27g | sodium: 80mg

Conclusion

I hope that I have inspired you to make changes to your way of eating. Following this diet is not too difficult and the benefits are mind-blowing. If it all seems a bit overwhelming, then start slowly and make gradual changes. As I said before, the goal is not to be perfect, it is to change the way you think about food.

Our bodies deserve to be treated with love and respect, and that is exactly what this diet will do for you. So, make the changes that are necessary, not for any other reason than you are worth it!

Appendix 1 Measurement Conversion Chart

VOLUME EQUIVALENTS(DRY)

US STANDARD	METRIC (APPROXIMATE)
1/8 teaspoon	0.5 mL
1/4 teaspoon	1 mL
1/2 teaspoon	2 mL
3/4 teaspoon	4 mL
1 teaspoon	5 mL
1 tablespoon	15 mL
1/4 cup	59 mL
1/2 cup	118 mL
3/4 cup	177 mL
1 cup	235 mL
2 cups	475 mL
3 cups	700 mL
4 cups	1 L

VOLUME EQUIVALENTS(LIQUID)

US STANDARD	US STANDARD (OUNCES)	METRIC (APPROXIMATE)
2 tablespoons	1 fl.oz.	30 mL
1/4 cup	2 fl.oz.	60 mL
1/2 cup	4 fl.oz.	120 mL
1 cup	8 fl.oz.	240 mL
1 1/2 cup	12 fl.oz.	355 mL
2 cups or 1 pint	16 fl.oz.	475 mL
4 cups or 1 quart	32 fl.oz.	1 L
1 gallon	128 fl.oz.	4 L

TEMPERATURES EQUIVALENTS

FAHRENHEIT(F)	CELSIUS(C) (APPROXIMATE)
225 °F	107 °C
250 °F	120 °C
275 °F	135 °C
300 °F	150 °C
325 °F	160 °C
350 °F	180 °C
375 °F	190 °C
400 °F	205 °C
425 °F	220 °C
450 °F	235 °C
475 °F	245 °C
500 °F	260 °C

WEIGHT EQUIVALENTS

US STANDARD	METRIC (APPROXIMATE)
1 ounce	28 g
2 ounces	57 g
5 ounces	142 g
10 ounces	284 g
15 ounces	425 g
16 ounces (1 pound)	455 g
1.5 pounds	680 g
2 pounds	907 g

Appendix 2 The Dirty Dozen and Clean Fifteen

The Environmental Working Group (EWG) is a nonprofit, nonpartisan organization dedicated to protecting human health and the environment Its mission is to empower people to live healthier lives in a healthier environment. This organization publishes an annual list of the twelve kinds of produce, in sequence, that have the highest amount of pesticide residue-the Dirty Dozen-as well as a list of the fifteen kinds of produce that have the least amount of pesticide residue-the Clean Fifteen.

THE DIRTY DOZEN

- The 2016 Dirty Dozen includes the following produce. These are considered among the year's most important produce to buy organic:

Strawberries	Spinach
Apples	Tomatoes
Nectarines	Bell peppers
Peaches	Cherry tomatoes
Celery	Cucumbers
Grapes	Kale/collard greens
Cherries	Hot peppers

- *The Dirty Dozen list contains two additional items kale/collard greens and hot peppers-because they tend to contain trace levels of highly hazardous pesticides.*

THE CLEAN FIFTEEN

- The least critical to buy organically are the Clean Fifteen list. The following are on the 2016 list:

Avocados	Papayas
Corn	Kiw
Pineapples	Eggplant
Cabbage	Honeydew
Sweet peas	Grapefruit
Onions	Cantaloupe
Asparagus	Cauliflower
Mangos	

- *Some of the sweet corn sold in the United States are made from genetically engineered (GE) seedstock. Buy organic varieties of these crops to avoid GE produce.*

Made in the USA
Coppell, TX
23 December 2021